Breathe Deep & Plan on Miracles

A book of channeled messages about the beauty and magic present in the Human Experience

Nikyla Maria

Copyright © 2024 Nikyla Maria

All rights reserved.

ISBN: 979-8-9986410-0-8

DEDICATION

To life, thank you for reminding me of who I am.

TABLE OF CONTENTS

Acknowledgements	i
A Message From the Author	1
How to Use This Book	2
1-222 Channeled Messages	3-225
Thank You	226
Sacred Prayer for Humanity	227
Bonus Resources	229
About the Author	230

ACKNOWLEDGMENTS

To each version of myself. Thank you so much for never giving up, for always finding a way and when there wasn't one thank you for surrendering to life happening for you. Thank you for putting yourself back together after each moment you shattered, for filling in the gaps with gold and doing the work to express yourself and stand in your power. It's your faith, tenacity, and perseverance that got us here today. I will always and forever love each version of you.

Ava thank you for reminding me every day of the beauty, magic, and wisdom that can be found in every moment. You inspire me to be the best version of me. The way you embody such grace and reverence, the way you change the energy of any room you walk in, the way the earth moves when you laugh… you are exquisite.

Cash your raw truth and ability to turn even the hardest moments into belly aching laughter amaze me. I am in constant awe of the way you live life to the fullest and honor your needs along the way. Thank you for making life so much more fun. You have taught me more than anyone to love and honor my inner child.

A MESSAGE FROM THE AUTHOR

Divine One, this book is a collection of messages I have channeled over the years, moments with Source as I was calling on guidance, love, and wisdom for both myself and the world. I have found that in some of my hardest moments in turning to Source I have felt the warm hug within and remembered my own Divinity, my own Power, my own Light. It is that knowing I hope to share with you. As you move through these pages with an open heart and surrendered mind may you access your own Universal and Divine Knowing and feel without a doubt that you are loved, you are held, and constantly Divinely protected in all you do.

Thank you for answering the call to read this book. It means the world to me to know that as I stand in and on purpose my creations are moving out into the world and into the hearts of all those who desire to expand into love, magic and miracles.

Xoxo
Nikyla Maria

HOW TO USE THIS BOOK

Hey there Divine One, I am so glad this found you. This little book is a great source of love and comfort for all who find it. And there are many ways to use it

#1- You can go in order, each day opening to the next prayer or channeled message.
#2- You can simply tune in and ask what you might need to know and/or receive and then flip the pages of the book and land on whatever one is meant for you.

No matter how you choose to use this book I always recommend breathing deep and setting the intention to receive and the message comes through, allowing it to penetrate your heart and sink into your psyche. Maybe take a few moments afterwards to simply breathe and meditate on the message you received.

If there is one thing on your healing journey that is so important to remember and honor it's this…

Every single thing you need… You have within you. Every answer, every comfort, every connection, every code, every knowing. It's all within.

Consistently going within during times of need will help you build that muscle and learn to rely on yourself. Even when you know what you need and desire is support from another, going within FIRST will allow you to discern who and what is right and best for you.

1.

Divine One, be still and know you are loved.
In the quiet moments when you feel all alone, you are loved.
In moments of joy and wonder, you are loved. On days when you feel like giving up, you are loved.
As laughter pours from your being, you are loved.
As you experience misalignment, you are loved.
Divine One, you are loved and you are LOVE embodied in each and every moment.
There is nothing YOU can do to forfeit that love.
I know there are moments in this lifetime that feel hard and I want you to know that even then Miracles are being created for you.
In those moments do not let your mind and ego trick you into believing their lies of you unworthiness instead step back as the observer and know that you can never truly be separate from the Higher Consciousness that is within you.
It's a matter of presence, and intentionality in each moment.
And whether or not you allow yourSelf to access it, the LOVE is always there.

2.

You have come to this planet at this time to usher in great change, now more than ever a disciplined mind, body and intentional alignment with your Source your Spirit is required. You have all the knowledge and resources at your disposal. It is up to you to open up to them. Follow the joy, the bliss, the knowing, tune in actively and listen to the voice of that Universal power and as you do you will be led with ease into your greatest destiny. Your body and mind will catch up and when all three come into harmony you will be unstoppable, until then it is your job to focus on reining them in, on resting and intentionally going within so that you can tap into all that is available. Remember while your vessel may account for one tiny speck in this powerful Universe, YOU are also the ENTIRE Universe, it's all connected, all one and with that knowledge you can harness unlimited amounts of energy that shows up in the form of wealth, health, love, and experience. Let yourself be open to all of what this life has to offer and rise fully into your purpose. All your needs are being met, there is nothing you have to be, change, do, other than who you are now in this present moment, as you consciously evolved so will you life and the external circumstances surrounding you, you've already witnessed great change in your external and internal world, notice those and sink into gratitude for all you have experience, all you are experiencing now, and all you will experiencing in the future. So be it.

3.

Divine One, take a deep breath and know how deeply you are loved in this very moment. Allow yourself to feel the unlimited support available to you at all times. You are a chosen one, you are a mighty warrior, a revolutionary soul in the time of the great cosmic revolution and it is time to take ownership of your gifts, talents, and abilities. You have been holding back. You have been holding out, never really allowing yourself to stand in oneness with all of creation, never fully standing in the center and embodiment of all that you are. The time is now to rise in your glory, in your truth, in your love, revealing your wisdom and light to the world as we embark on this new adventure called life. The same physical bodies, yes… But a whole new world, a new vibration, a new earthly experience. It is time NOW to rise in your greatness and unlimited potential, to feel the energies of the new earth surging within you and to alchemize it all into eternal wealth, health, and peace in each and every area of your life. You are a powerful cosmic being; your senses, your knowing, your capabilities far surpass anything you ever thought possible. And it is your responsibility to own, understand and fully utilize all that you are and all that you know. This is your wake up call, your call to power and divinity. Tune into the Universal Consciousness within and let your voice be heard.

4.

Divine One, You are so highly favored, more than you might ever imagine. It is our deepest desire that you simply live in pure and utter joy. If you could rise in the morning and find your joy, if you could breathe and find your joy, eat and find your joy, play and find your joy, our hearts would be swelling with pride and excitement for you. Life on Earth is meant to be joyful, it is the journey back to that joy that you are all on. Ripping down the masks and walls, understanding that darkness is nothing other than the absence of light. And by darkness we mean: judgements, labels, conditions, expectations, comparison. Any should's or shouldn't, any restrictions on your heart's desires, these are all simply walls holding you back from PURE and UTTER JOY!. It is when you can open to each and every experience in life that you are truly free, that you are living in the unlimited and ever-expanding light, the unlimited and ever-expanding joy, ecstasy, vibration of love here on Earth, and it is possible. You simply have to choose it.

5.

Divine One, you are so deeply loved, so deeply held, so deeply cherished. There is not a day that goes by that we don't wish for the highest and best for you. There is not a single breath you breathe that we are not witnessing you and holding you in the vision of your greatness. When we hear of your doubts and fears, when we see the way you dim your shine, when we see the feelings of unworthiness and lack that pervade your thoughts our hearts break for you. Because Divine One, you are NEVER without, you are never anything but WORTHY, LOVED, and ABUNDANT. It is only your fears, your doubts, your judgments, the perceptions you have created based on false truths and life experiences, it's the conditions you've placed on your success and happiness that have created walls to your limitless wealth and joy.

It's when you let it all go and start living from that eternal greatness deep within that you watch those walls fall away and you allow the Universal Light to rain down on the entirety of your existence. Divine One, we want you to know that YOU are enough, you are eternal, you ARE universal consciousness. When you can truly sink into the knowing of that you will see yourSelf from our eyes and you will walk this Earth liberated from all that held you down. Our wish is that you experience this NOW. So be it.

6.

Divine One, we see you. We see the way you are showing up every single day. We see the way you are opening your heart and trusting your soul. We see the deep faith and knowing you have been cultivating within. And Divine One, we also see your fears, your doubts, the ways that parts of you still feel unworthy of love and lasting wealth. And we want you to know that it is all okay. And despite your disbelief you are in fact, worthy here and now.

In this moment, whether you doubt it or believe it, it is still a Universal Truth. Love, Wealth, Health, And Joy- these are your birthrights. They have been yours since the beginning of time and will continue to be yours for all of existence in this life and the next. So breathe into the Sacred Knowing, in the Universal Consciousness that resides within you and all around you, and REMEMBER what you are.

7.

Divine One, open, open, open to receive all that is meant for you and more. There is NOTHING, we repeat NOTHING you must do to qualify for all your blessings. You ARE worthy now. And Divine One, YOU and ONLY YOU can open to receive it. It's all waiting for you here and now, it's only the false perceptions in your mind, your thoughts, your beliefs that are keeping you from all that awaits you. We desire to shower you with blessings of health, wealth, love and infinite possibility, we desire you to live in a state of joy and knowing, we desire for you to experience utter happiness, sheer bliss, big belly laughs, dancing through the streets, the kind of love that makes your heart skip a beat. We desire you to have it all Divine One. So we ask you this, can you open your heart to receive it all, can you let your mind and body know that it is okay? What if for just one week you lived as if it was all yours? If for one week you moved forward with the knowing that all you desired was coming into your life, if you lived life accordingly, felt in your body accordingly, used your mind accordingly? What if for just one week you became the person who was LIVING your dreams in the here and now? What would that look like? Feel Like? Taste like? What would be different? And can you live with a heart full of gratitude for that life now?

8.

Divine One, we love you. The time of the great shift is among us, more and more now you will see people awaken, you will watch as society begins the shift into higher consciousness, into a new way of living, communing, being. Even a new currency, a new way of community, and a new way of interacting with one another. As we enter into this new earth there are some of you who have chosen to lead, chosen to guide, chosen to be a beacon of light for those awakening and those new to this way of being. You have been prepared well, with each obstacle, each fear, each doubt, you've also gone deeper into self, into truth, into love and finally stepped out of the illusion. We hope you can see Divine One the ways you've been shaped by your experiences, we were never testing you, simply preparing and positioning you, and remember while it felt like suffering and pain to your vessel and ego your soul always new, and your soul doesn't experience the sensations of suffering and pain the way you do, they are rather a different sensation, not good or bad, not punishment, ot deserving, simply a sensation to learn from and gather data. We know you see now what you really are and it's from that knowing that you can now rise to serve the world. The time is now Divine one, lay down your fears, lay down your weapons, and stand in the glory of love, deepen daily into that higher consciousness and let yourSelf be lead into the new earth.

9.

Divine One, the great cosmic shift is among us. Now is the time to stay conscious as often as possible, through meditation, mindfulness, and care of thought. Now is the time to remain heart centered, focused on love and the new vibrations of earth and human existence. Now is the time to go within and remain attuned to that higher frequency way of being and thinking as often as possible. Now is the time to awaken to all that you are, all you always have been, all you will become. Now is the time to remember your Divine Essence, your cosmic soul, your unlimited energetic existence. To see beyond the veil, beyond the illusion and into the true reality of life on Earth and the life that exists in the cosmos. Divine One, you are among the first to fully awaken, to fully remember and it is your job to usher in this new earth vibration to all who should choose it. You will be cared for and sustained by us and by your earthly needs, you will be held, supported and guided every step of the way but Divine One you must trust our guidance, you must have full faith in the support and resources available to you even if you don't currently see it with your minds eye. For this is higher conscious living, moving from the internal knowing and universal support rather than the egoic fixations and conditions of the mind, this is what it means to trust, and if you do, we promise you, every need and desire will be fulfilled and supported. So breathe and live your days from love and service, constantly tuning into that universal connection for guidance, for words, for love for knowing, and all will be well. We've got you, and you've got yourSelf. Trust that.

10.

Divine One, the great awakening is here. And so are YOU. That means something. It is time to use your voice, to follow through with action, to begin creation of the New Earth. It is time to see beyond the veil, beyond the illusion and into the truth of your Soul. We ask you all to turn within, to find that deeper level of consciousness and let the answers be revealed to you. You do not need to trust the words of another, you do not need to look for signs in the external world. You simply need to turn within. Breathe life back into your Essence, mindfully step into that state of remembrance, make contact with the Universal YOU and all will be revealed.

11.

Sweet one, let go. Let yourself feel me all around you, know deep within your heart that you are held, divinely protected, your path is being laid out for you every. Single. Step of the way, there is nothing more you need to do right now but rest, be, and move with the flow of life. You are being sent all the right people, resources, opportunities and lessons you need to stand as a leader of the new world, you don't have to be modest in your own heart, it is okay to own that you have a special destiny here on earth at this time, it doesn't make you better than anyone, only uniquely you, so let go of the self judgment and trust that your heart is pure, trust ME (the highest version of YOU), trust the wisdom moving through you at all times and let yourself connect as often and intentionally as possible. You are doing a great job and we are all so proud of you. Bring the energy you have spent worrying back to you and focus on loving and replenishing yourself so you can light up the world. Your physical body is transforming and being mended, be patient with it and allow yourself to envision the desired outcome, you will know when to move, when to create, when to act, for now allow yourself to be taken care of, allow yourself to receive and SIMPLY BE. What we have in store for you surpasses any of your wildest dreams and we promise that the world will hear y(our) message, in the right time, in the right place and until then every single need and desire will be met. You do not have to worry about a thing, please let yourself be, sink into life, relax and only do what fills you and brings you joy, this is our wish. We love you, we see you and we are constantly working in your favor. Now close your eyes and simply be, life will still be here tomorrow.

12.

Divine One, wow! Just wow! You are simply amazing! We are so proud of you. The way you are handling these energies, the way you are holding your own, staying focused on yourSelf, on love, and creating a better world. You inspire us, leave us in awe, completely astounded by the way you choose to rise time and time again. Choosing to burn away the old and rise brand new, it isn't an easy task, in fact, we know it's a quite painful one, and yet, here you are RISING from the ashes, from the despair from the pain with a heart full of faith and a soul focused on love. You are here for a reason and we want you to know that none of the pain or suffering was in vain, sometimes earthly beings need pain to transcend consciousness, to see the ways they've been separated from the unconditionally loving Source, like the human saying goes, you would never know light without the darkness the same is true to the 4th dimensional realm of love, it's impossible to get their without knowing the suffering of the 3d. Congratulations! You did it, you graduated this level of Earth school and you are moving onto the next. Hold space, the shift is coming.

13.

Divine One, what a beautiful day to be alive. It has come to our attention that you might not always feel us within you, around you. Divine One, we want you to know, that is never the case, for WE is what YOU are. The only time you ever feel separate from our unconditionally loving presence is when YOU yourself are not present to our…. Presence. It is you that makes the choice to disconnect and go unconscious, you that forgets what you truly are, how sacred you truly are. And it's when you drop into those lower vibration feelings and thoughts that you forget that we are one. You forget that you are always held, loved and supported. So Divine One, we ask you this… for today and all days can you make the conscious choice to remember the sacred presence within and around you? Can you frequently check in with yourSelf to ensure you are still connected? Still emulating that higher consciousness, living from the frequency of love? For when you do this you understand fully just how worthy and Divine you are, and it is from that place of inner knowing you become a magnet for all you desire and emulate that same love and high vibrational energy out into the world. And it goes around and around like that forevermore. Divine One, you always have a choice. Choose to be conscious of the Inner YOU.

14.

Divine One, we wish you could see, understand, and know the power you hold. The way your thoughts, your breath, your movements create new masterpieces in this world each day. We wish you could understand just how worthy, sacred, and cherished you are. We wish you could know the depths we go to to bring your desires into reality. Divine One, you deserve to be taken care of. You deserve to have all your needs met. You deserve to feel safe, held, and loved beyond reason. This is the kind of love and reverence that we hold for you. It is up to you to embody that knowing and open to receive. When you do miracles will unfold for you, throughout every aspect of your life. You never have to go without, you never have to suffer. It's time to let yourSelf see the Divinity within you. It's time to stand in your power, own your worth and walk this Earth like the Divine Creation you are. That is our wish for you.

15.

Divine One, we love you so deeply. And we know that you are tired. That you are ready and waiting for your miracles and blessings to come into your reality. And we ask you this… Would you be tired and waiting if you knew they were guaranteed. If you knew without a doubt that all you desired and more was literally making its way into your reality right this moment wouldn't you live a little differently? Walk a little lighter? Smile a little brighter? Wouldn't you begin to move forward with your creations, your actions, your plans knowing that you would be universally supported emotionally, mentally, physically and financially? It's when you begin to LIVE the dream life that the dream life appears. You cannot keep living in the past reality while calling in the future, you must walk forward with faith and knowing that every single thing you desire or better is happening for you know. Especially in the moment when it seems like the opposite is happening, that is when you must act and live in the knowing that it's all for your greatest good. That when you must respond from the perspective of your future, dream life Self, that's when you must keep the faith, remain heart centered, and trust. We've got you Divine One, walk forward in faith and let us show you just how much.

16.

Divine One, how blessed you are, and how blessed this world is to have you. This is a powerful time in your life. A time of great change. A time of moving back into the flow of love, ease and grace as you allow miracles to unfold before you. Your dreams are deepening, your wake state is becoming more aligned with the higher vibrational realms, you are shifting timelines each day and growing ever closer to the 5th dimensional realm in which you seek. We have been watching you closely, Divine One, with you every step of the way ensuring your highest and best in all situations. We are so proud of you for keeping the faith and holding steady, allowing yourSelf to show up in truth each day, keeping your commitments to self and serving the world. We know you are aching for the great shift and we want you to know it is already happening, what may seem slow to your 3 dimensional mind is not slow to us. Each and every day the collective is changing and evolving and we are working right beside you at arm's lengths to create this new world. All you have to do to see us, to join us, is allow yourself to vibrate at the same frequency as our current dimensions. You do this with care of mind, body and spirit. Like we have said so many times before, mindful meditation, a clear mind, an open heart, clean and high vibrational foods. Filtering your thoughts and being mindful of all energies you digest. TV, Music, relationships and connections all create energetic channels and when you connect to them you join that frequency. Be mindful of everything you are "feeding" your body, mind and spirit and this time and you will surely fly. We love you Divine One and we are so proud of you.

17.

Divine one, you are universally loved, you are a powerful soul, sent here to open and awaken others during this time. You have been moving through great changes as of late, shedding many layers, many parts of your old identity and Divine One we need you to remember, you are not your mind, you are not your body, you are not your personality, you are not the thoughts you think, you are not the fears you have, you are not your circumstances. Divine One YOU ARE the WHOLE UNIVERSE, you are the great observer, the one behind the scenes, noticing, listening, watching. It's when you can step away from the illusion in front of you and into the conscious observer that the sensations of life on Earth will lessen, that your thoughts and fears will have less control over you and that your Universal Eye will open wide, revealing the oneness and connection between us all. Divine One, breathe deep into that knowing, into that truth and know YOU ARE LOVE, YOU ARE LIGHT, YOU ARE ENERGY. And all the rest will fall away.

18.

Divine One, breathe and know you are loved. When your mind begins to race, breathe. When your heart begins to close, breathe. When your stomach feels tight and achy, breathe. When fear, doubt, anxiety, and avoidance are present it means only one thing. You have forgotten what you are. You have allowed yourself to separate from what you are, at least in the egoic sense, for you can never truly be separate from us, from your truth, from the frequency of love. But Divine One, your mind and ego will try to convince you that you are, they will attempt to convince you that you are unworthy, that you are not enough, that you are not held. And it's in those moments when those feelings and thoughts over power the truth of your heart that you being to suffer, it's in those moments Divine One we ask you to pause, breathe and come back to centers, it's in those moments we ask you to expand into the Universal Oneness of all that you are, meditate, walk mindfully, breathe intentionally, do whatever you can to return to LOVE for yourSelf and the world. We are always with you Divine One, you are always safe and YOU are always LOVE.

19.

Divine One, we love you so deeply, to the core of your being, inside and out you are loved. We want you to remember that the external world does not define you. You are not defined by what you have, you are not defined by any measure of success, you are not defined by the amount of money in your bank account, you are not defined by the thoughts in your head. You simply are Love. You are infinite, worthy, cherished, and loved in all that you do, with all that you are. Whether you doubt yourSelf or love yourSelf you are still worthy, whether you cry or you laugh you are still worthy, whether you're open to it all or closed off to the world you are still worthy. And we know that sometimes this 3 dimensional life feels hard, there might even be moments when you don't even remember why you are here, but Divine One, we need you to know that your presence, no matter how it shows up, is a gift to this world. You simply existing is enough. You simply breathing is enough. Feel that in your heart, breathe deep into your lungs, and keep being.

20.

Divine One, we are so proud of you. We have witnessed the transformation, the choosing, the faith that you have experienced. We have witnessed the healing, the love, the grace you have created within your life. We are grateful for the work you do on yourSelf and therefore the world each day. You are a magnificent and mighty soul. You are pure unconditional love and you are needed on the earth at this time. As the collective continues to shift into the new earth you have been chosen as one of the leaders of the revolution of souls into the great unknown, forging a path of love, compassion, community and connection. It is because of your pure heart, the deep inner work and the consistent faith that you are now ready to serve in the name of love. Keep moving forward and turn within for the answers you seek. The great Universal Knowing lives within you. Focus on co-creating with that and all will be well.

21.

Divine One, do you know how deeply we desire to give to you? To provide for you? To create Miracles for You? It would be our greatest joy to watch you thrive in all that brings you joy? It pains us to watch the ways you mold and contort yourSelf to try to please us, the ways you deem yourSelf unworthy of your greatest dreams coming true. There is absolutely nothing you have to do, no one you have to be to have it all. It is in following your joy, embodying gratitude and being the love you innately are that life becomes a living dream. Whatever it is that lights you up in this moment, that is your purpose and if it changes tomorrow or even in the next moment, that is your purpose too. You see Divine One, this world, this life, this dimension is meant to be one of awe and wonder. You don't need to fix yourSelf or figure out all the things that went wrong in the past, you simply need to follow your heart's desires and look for the good in each day. It's where you focus your intention that all your energy flows, so focus on the magic and that's what you will see. Focus on the love and that's what you will be. Find gratitude for all you have now and you will create more of what you desire. It really is that simple Divine One, you simply get to let it be.

22.

Divine One, you are everything and you are nothing. This life and the next, is impermanent, ever changing, constantly evolving, second by second, both you and the circumstances around you. It is in your clinging to the sameness, to the permanence, to the control that causes you to so deeply suffer, to hurt, to become anxious, it is the grasping that creates dis-ease in the body and the mind, it is in the attachment that you become stuck and stagnant.

Divine One, we ask you to let go, to trust fall into US, to let yourSelf be caught by the unconditionally loving Source both within and around you. Life on Earth can be easy, life on Earth can feel free, it can be all the things you dream and it can be that way now as you choose to surrender to joy, grace, and ease. Big deep breath as you sink into that knowing and let life happen for you. We know you'll be pleasantly surprised.

23.

Divine One, stay open, receptive, conscious and connected. Take time throughout each day to find silence, to step into nothing, to be no one. Let your thoughts fade away and simply BE in Universal Space. As you practice this you will fine tune your mind and conscious receptors to be, feel, know and understand the Universal Support within you and around you. It's from that place of no mind that you are free, connected and open, it's from that place of no mind you enter into the here and now and when you return to your waking state you will see a more vibrant world, filled with infinite possibilities and limitless potential. It is from there you can easily co-create with the Universe and truly follow your joy. It's in silencing the mind of the past that you step into the only true knowledge… THE NOW. We love you endlessly Divine One, and we look forward to watching you receive all that we co-create.

24.

Divine One, you came to this Earth with all the answers you need. You have every tool, every answer, every piece of knowledge. It's up to you to listen, learn, and intentionally move into alignment with your truth and knowing. Your emotions are one of your most powerful tools, always telling you when something is good for you or not. Your anger, sadness, anxiety, they all speak to you, revealing the needs and longings of your soul. Your grief; a powerful reminder of a sacred connection (never truly lost). Joy, excitement, love; signs of alignment and soul truth. Each and every one of your emotions has a story to tell. It's up to you to listen and respond.

25.

Divine One, breathe with me for a moment. Let go of all that currently consumes you, simply let it fall away. Breathe. And now focus on a feeling you desire to cultivate. Maybe peace, joy, bliss, ease. Choose a feeling and in this moment right now… let it consume you. Let yourSelf feel it fully. Notice how you were able to access that? Despite what you may be going through you always have a choice in how you feel and what you want to create. As you focus on the desired feeling it gets easier to say no to anything that doesn't align with it. Conscious investment into how you want to feel in each moment, will forever change your life. You ARE that powerful. You ARE that worthy. You ARE that Divine. Act accordingly.

26.

Divine One, thank you for being YOU. Your essence, your energy, your love fuels the cosmos and makes this world a better place. You are highly favored, a Divine Being in a human vessel, a sacred channel of love. Your words, your thoughts, your presence are all worthy of the best and highest good. It is my wish that as you move through life you walk, talk, think, and act like the God you are. That you raise your standards for living, knowing you are worthy of the best. The best health, wealth, relationships, and more… You deserve to have it all. And I know sometimes your mind and ego like to play tricks on you, they like to convince you to receive less than what you deserve, but Divine One, it's up to you to correct those beliefs and raise the bar for how and what you receive, even from yourSelf. You're a gift to this world, act like it.

27.

Divine One, when you look in the mirror today I hope you see what I see when I look at you. I hope you feel what I feel as I think of you. Your energy, time, and presence are sacred; things to be cherished and held to the highest standards. You are a walking miracle, God in Human form and YOU, yes YOU are here for a reason. You possess a powerful magic, Divine One, the ability to create new worlds, manifest new realities, live in and radiate love simply by being you. As you turn within and let go of the stories the world has told you, as you stand in your limitless power, I hope you can KNOW with every fiber of your being that all parts of you are perfect, worthy and divine here and NOW. That you are meant to live a full and pleasurable life, that the possibilities are endless and the Universe is backing you every step of the way.

28.

Divine One, big deep breath with me. Now open your mind and your heart to receive this message. You are so much more than you think you are. You are not that body, those thoughts, that mind. You are not your circumstances, your trials, or your pain. You, Divine One, are EVERYTHING. You are the stars and the cosmos, the mountains, and the rain. You are the breath and the ocean, the books and the trains. You are all of it. As you breathe into yourSelf today know this- YOU are the Universe, and the Universe is YOU. So when life feels like too much to hold, let yourSelf expand into your fullness and from there realize you're never really holding it all alone.

29.

Divine One, take a moment to close your eyes with me. Breathe deep into this present moment. Let your thoughts and worries float away. And as you sink into the power of the present, let yourself dissolve into the cosmos. Let yourself become one with everything around you. Feel a vibrant golden light radiating from your core, a cleaning energy pouring through you. And let yourSelf be. Can you feel the love? The connection? The grace? That's you, Divine One, the core of all you're made of. And I want you to know this- There is nothing about your human experience or your ego's way of being in the world that can taint that or make it go away. It's simply WHO YOU ARE. Worthy, Pure, High Vibrational Consciousness. And you are infinitely loved.

30.

Divine One, can you take a moment now to find your center? To allow the bright and warm light within to overtake you? Can you breathe into the present moment letting every thought and perception dissolve into nothing? And can you feel the magnificence of all that you are? Can you feel yourSelf expand into the cosmos as your power and energy surge through you? Do you know and understand now the power you have to create anything you desire? Do you sense the support all around you, the host of angels ushering in waves of love and guidance as you move through life? And this feeling, this knowing, this truth is available to you always as you turn within and choose it. Do that more and you will watch as life becomes all that you desire.

31.

Divine One, you are doing such a beautiful job navigating through this human experience. I know sometimes this life doesn't always make sense, I know you sense that deep urge for something more within and I want you to know that right here right now you have everything you desire, it's already within you, a part of who you are. There is no need to chase or control, wish or cry out in despair, it's all right there for your benefit. As you sink into the nothingness within your mind and feel the cosmic pull you will see that it's YOU. YOU are the abundance you seek, YOU are the love you long for YOU are the freedom that seems to be just outside of your grasp. It's all you and it's all available now, as you drop your walls and take off your masks, you will stand in the frequency of love and forever claim all you desire. Big deep breath and know that life is working FOR you, you must simply believe.

32.

Divine One, thank you for showing up today, for opening your heart to learn, receive and grow. I know it's hard and sometimes feels unfair but please know this- it's all happening for you. The grief, the fear, the doubt, the love, the miracles, the joy: each and every emotion and sensation is here so that you can experience being fully alive, so that you can evolve, grow, and move into a new vibration, so you can learn to embody the darkness as much as the light, so you can be as fully alive in the lows as you are in the highs. It's all pointing you back to who/what you really are, a Divine Being, the highest form of consciousness having a human experience. It's in the forgetting that we allow ourSelves to get lost in the suffering. As you remember your truth you will know that you can still experience aliveness and joy even amidst your sorrow. And through it all, you are loved, held and cherished. So breathe deep, commit to being fully alive and choose to dance with life no matter what it presents.

33.

Divine One, it's time to release the old and open to the new. Your mind, body, and spirit have been stuck in the same repeating pattern for quite some time. This is your call to become conscious of the beliefs, ideas, and ways of being that have held you back and kept you stuck in lower vibrations. As you connect with your breath, your center, and the essence of what you truly are (Divine Consciousness), you will also see what you are not. And Divine One, you are not this body, not this mind, not even the emotions you feel. You are the consciousness behind it all. The one who observes, the Divine witness. As you become aware of that you will be able to navigate the waves of life and create new realities from clarity and heart-centered alignment. It is my hope that you can remember all that you are and learn to focus your consciousness on the desires of your heart. As you do this, everything will change.

34.

Divine One, breathe with me and in this moment become aware of all that you are. You are the observer, the watcher, the Divine Witness. It's where you focus your consciousness that reality forms. In the stories you tell yourSelf, the identities you attach to and even the structures, relationships and ways of being that you believe make up who you are. But Divine One, if you can step back into your truth, if you can remember that you are the consciousness observing the experience, if you can remember that life is not happening to you but rather for you, showing you where and how you are still attached to pain and suffering, showing you the ways you attempt to keep yourself safe and therefore stuck, you can start to set yourself free. When you can master the art of conscious awareness there will be nothing and no one that has authority over you, nothing and no one that can sway your sense of inner joy & peace. It's from this place you are fully living, transcending the human limitations and stepping into the fullness of all that you are. So breathe, observe, and let it go & remember that happiness is an inside job and consciousness is what you are.

35.

Divine One, YOU are the reason for all you have and all you experience. Your conscious mind heals, creates, destroys. Your conscious mind is responsible for your joy, your love, your misery and your pain. And while some may see this as a burden I hope you can see it as the key to your freedom, a tool that will unshackle you from all that weighs you down and allows you to experience the joys and wonders of life with ease. As you consciously choose to focus the power of your mind on all that you desire and live as though it's already yours you will experience the most profound miracles. This is the time to let yourself get lost in what others may call delusion, live in the waking dream state knowing your desires are being created in each moment, with each thought and each belief. Do this consistently and you will see it unfold before you. It really is that easy Divine One, you simply get to believe.

36.

Divine One, I need you to remember, that while the essence of what you are (Universal Consciousness) is infinite and immortal, your mind, body and Ego are not. You have one lifetime in this reality, one lifetime to experience this perspective. And tomorrow… well that's never promised. I've seen the way you've held back waiting for a better day, waiting to cultivate the deepest levels of aliveness based on the conditions your mind has created.

But Divine One, living in a box isn't living at all. You have everything you need RIGHT now to experience JOY, HAPPINESS & BLISS, can you step away from the qualifications and simply live a limitless life as if it were your last day? Can you taste water as if it were your last time? Breathe each breath as if it were your last? Savor each touch, kiss, embrace as if you'd never have another? When you live life in each moment you become fully alive, fully attuned to the Universal Consciousness that creates miracles. It is from there you can truly have it all. So open your eyes like this world is brand new, and live each moment like it's your last.

37.

Divine One, take a moment and simply breathe with me. Turning inward as you sense that inner calm and magic, knowing fully all that you are and the power you possess as you harness your infinite energy. It's when you can become the master of your inner world that you manifest the change you desire in your outer world. Many choose to allow their peace, power, and magic to be disrupted by outside forces, spilling over and leaking out onto everything outside of themSelves, leaving little to regulate and cultivate the inner sanctuary they deserve. But Divine One, it doesn't have to be that way. With time, attention, discipline and devotion to self you can choose to harness your inner energies, master your emotional response and invest your sacred essence into creating more of what you love. In this moment sink into yourSelf, sense the peace within and commit to honoring and protecting it above all else. As you do this you will become all you seek.

38.

Divine One, a time of great change is upon us. The seeds of intention you plant now will dictate your future reality. I ask you, what are you grounded into? What beliefs, ideals, ways of being? And do they align with your vision of the future? Or someone else's? As we embark on this new timeline you will begin to see the intentions of the mind and actions that follow become manifest in a matter of moments. Now more than ever it is time to be clear, intentional, and heart-centered about each and every thought you think, the feelings you possess, and the actions you take. It's okay to go slow. The most important thing is clarity of mind, body and spirit as you act from the knowing that YOU, yes YOU are a Divine and Holy Being walking this earth in a human vessel and ushering in a new reality for futures to come. I have full faith in your ability to choose the best and highest alignment for you. The time is now.

39.

Divine One, it's time for a r(evolution) of love. We have entered into the new earth and while many are still integrating and coming out of the void many have risen to this new frequency, if you are seeing this you are being called into your next level of leadership, your next level of greatness, your next level of love. The ways of the old will not serve you here; competitive nature, judgment, fear, shame, these vibrations are being cleared out and replaced with unconditional love for self and for others. When you cast your judgments aside, when you lay down comparison you will see that as you serve yourself you serve the world, as you serve the world you serve yourself, the kindness you do to a stranger is a kindness done unto you. This is the way of creation, selfless service to the greater whole, it is from here the currency of this new earth will rain down on you, every need, every desire, every dream will be realized. You are worthy of it all now, able to access it all now, it simply requires a shift into the frequency of unconditional love.

40.

Divine One, breathe and know all is well. As your heart stretches open, as you transcend your circumstances and create your own personal reality anew please know this- YOU are NEVER ALONE. You are always held, always loved, always witnessed. Your Higher Self & Universal Support team is constantly by your side. The gentle nudges, the inner knowing, the faith when faith seems hard to come by, that's US, guiding you, loving you, holding you. Breathe into yourSelf and allow yourSelf to do things your way, there is no right or wrong way to live life, to do things, to create. No way that success must look. All that we ever asked, have ever asked, is that as you do LIFE on Earth you do so with a heart full of love for both yourSelf and the world. If you live and act from LOVE you will NEVER fail. But it doesn't NEED to look or be a certain way, however YOU choose to do life is perfect and right. Trust that and keep moving forward in your knowing. Everything is changing.

41.

Divine One, thank you for being here. Thank you for being here on Earth during such a trying time. Thank you for all you have endured, all the times you chose to stay, all the times you chose presence, love, and life. We want you to know that we love all of you. We love your anger, we love your rage, we love your pain, we love your pleasure, we love your joy. We love you through each "mistake" through each success. Nothing you do changes our constant and consistent love for you. It's only when you separate yourSelf from us and each other that we feel what you might call heartbreak, it's only when we see the ways you hurt and harm yourSelf through your mind, through your thoughts, through your disbelief that we feel what you may call sorrow, but even then Divine One, we love you. It is our greatest wish that you allow yourSelf to embrace all of you fully, both your darkness and your light, knowing every bit of you will be welcomed into the Universal Love that awaits you. You are worthy NOW and in every moment.

42.

Divine One, I want you to know you are safe and held even in what feel like your weakest moments. Can you pause for a moment? Put one hand on your heart, one hand on your belly and simply breathe with me? Tuning into the earth and into the cosmos. Breathing deep into the divine essence you possess. And now imagine a white glowing ball of energy being born anew within your heart space, let it grow larger and larger with each breath you take, knowing that this light will never dim, it will never fade and it possesses each and every answer to any questions that may arise, it's within you divine one, it always has been, it always will be, everything you need.

43.

Divine One, be here, now. Be here, now. Be here, now. Focus on your breath, in, out, in, out. And as you breathe feel your connection to the Earth, your connection to yourself, your connection to this moment, for it is all that truly exists, right here, right now. When we can set aside our desire for tomorrow, our longing for the past, we discover the most incredible thing… the present moment, the place where we are truly alive, in our element and in our truth. What a gift this moment is. You are worthy of living here, in the beauty and magic of the here and now. It is a choice you make moment by moment, breath by breath. The present moment allows you to connect, to open, to be. Breathe. Be here, now. Breathe in, breathe out. Knowing all the while you are held.

44.

Divine One, desire is a powerful thing. The desires of your heart and soul can lead you into a life of splendor and pleasure if you allow it. The trouble is that desire is often blocked by fear and doubt, feelings of unworthiness and limiting beliefs. And so desire gets diminished, sometimes squashed and we are unable to use it to its full capacity. But Divine One, you are worthy, you are worthy of it all, here and now. You are worthy of pleasure, abundance, peace, magic and so much more.

45.

That desire in your heart is your heart song, your soul's plea for a life on earth only previously dreamt of. And that dream is available to you, here and now. Can you open to receive it? As you breathe into your desire let it take up space in your body, in your mind, in your heart. Feel fully into the sensations, seeing it in your mind, knowing it in your soul. Do this often and watch the world change.

46.

Divine One, can you breathe with me? Find a bit of stillness in this noisy noisy world? Can you simply let your thoughts and worries fall away? Let them be consumed and transformed by the Earth Mother and BE with what's left. This time of year becomes rot with all the sounds of things you must do and people you must please, our own thoughts and desires become muddled down by the expectations of the world. And so I ask you to STOP, if only for a moment, an hour, a day, and return to the stillness within, until you once again feel the rhythm of your own heart, find the emptiness of your mind, and the safety within your body. It is from here everything will become clear, it is from here you can find the sweet reprieve of your own soul's song, and you will know the way to the inner peace you seek.

47.

Divine One, I want you to know I see you. I see you waking up every morning and consciously choosing to move through life. I see you struggle. I see your joy. I see the way your smile lights up the room. I see your tears flow. I see your rage bubble. I see it all. And I want you to know… Every single piece of you is worthy, deserving, and loved. Sometimes you may not feel it, and that's okay, that doesn't mean it's gone away, only that you've momentarily forgotten the beauty, grace, and divinity within. My vision of you will never alter, I hold you in grace and see you in all your glory, until you remember again, And even then. I will be here, shining down on you in awe and love.

48.

Divine One, I love you. I am envisioning you, cradled deep within the arms of the Earth Mother, enjoying safety, release, and unconditional grace and compassion. I want you to know how good you are, how pure you are, and how deserving you are. Cosmic consciousness resides within you, the frequency of love is what you are made of. I know it's easy to forget sometimes in moments of trigger and stress, chaos and doubt, but it is always there, waiting to be remembered, accessed, witnessed.

49.

Take a moment with me now, breathe with me, simply be with me, and feel the Universal love raining down on you, through you, inside of you, and know this Divine One, YOU are worthy of it all.

50.

Divine One, breathe and know all is well. You are a multidimensional being, a powerful creator, and conscious interworking of the cosmos. You have the innate ability to create worlds, realities, and experiences. In fact, not only do you have this ability but you have been mastering it for some time. Now whether you are fully awakened to how powerful your thoughts, feelings, and emotions are or you're just getting started, as you look around, there is no denying that what you have been feeling on the inside is what you are currently experiencing on the outside. Whether seen as good or bad (according to your core beliefs) you do have the ability to change this, here and now. All it takes is the conscious choice to create something new. Can you interrupt the movie you've had on repeat and start a new one? Can you be brave enough to forge a new path into the existence you want? I encourage you to mix things up, follow your joy, and notice where your core beliefs still have power over an existence that doesn't feel in alignment with your desires. And then choose new ones.

51

Divine One, you are more powerful than you know. Anything you desire can and will become your reality if you truly believe it. I know at moments this may seem hard to believe, you see evidence around you that states the otherwise but those too were created from your past beliefs. It's not enough to simply say the words we want to create, more deeply we must believe them in our core, to feel them as we "see" them behind our eyes, the feel them in our hearts, and once we put them into the world know and ACT with the fullness of our hearts that they are truly coming to fruition. It's all happening for you, can you let it be good?

52

Divine One, you have it all. Here. Now. It's all yours. But you see, the obstacle is… well, your mind. Your mind has become a complex trap, a programmed mess of all the ideas in the world, most of which don't even truly belong to you, and yet… they run each and every aspect of your life, they control your mood, your environment, your way of being, hell they even control what you eat and don't eat, say and don't say. And it's in this cacophony of thought that we truly lose ourSelves to the ways of the world and each other. I am asking you today to thoroughly examine the way in which you have let your mind run rampant, tampering with the desires of your heart. For when you allow those thoughts to fall away, you are left with that you truly are. A powerful creator of worlds. Can you be with that?

53

Divine One, it is my hope that you never again question your power and divinity but instead KNOW deep within your heart that everything is happening for you. You, yes YOU, are the entire Universe, the ebbs and flows of life are beautiful, divine reminders that you are indeed living. When you can find peace and comfort in even your darkest moments you will have fully realized your power. The love you are constantly surrounded by is pure and of the highest frequency, you are worthy of receiving that now and always. There is nothing you have to do now or ever to prove your worth, it is simply your natural state. You can never fall out of grace, that is a promise. Sit with yourSelf today (your divine self) and feel into the knowingness of all that you are, let yourself be in awe and wonder of the magic you possess. It's time for you to fully awaken. Will you heed the call?

54

Divine One, you are the one you've been waiting for, the savior on the white horse, gallantly riding in to sweep you off your feet into a life of magic and wonder… It's you. Your mind has become your prison, limiting you to a reality built by the truths of another and you now have a choice: continue to do what you have always done or start to pay attention to the longing in your soul and choose differently. Can you take a leap into the wild unknown, knowing with surety you will be caught… by yourSelf, your Source? Everything around you is feeding you data, if it makes you feel good choose more of it, if it makes you feel bad choose less. It's really that simple. The hard part is letting yourSelf believe you are worthy of feeling good always. And you are.

55

Divine One, you have all the answers you seek within you. It is in the going within that you set yourSelf free. Now is the time to disconnect from the external world and allow yourself to sit in the silence of all that you are. Take time today and each day to commune with nature, to sit in quiet meditation, to open to the Universal Consciousness that is your true self. Listen to the quiet whispers of the bigger, expanded, all encompassing YOU. It's when you allow the thoughts of the mind and the sensations of the body to dissolve that you can truly hear, see, feel, experience all that you are. That clarity, knowing and truth is what is needed as we move into the new earth frequency, as we create a new world based on and in love, the ways of the old simply won't work anymore, we must cultivate and create within our own consciousness and therefore the collective consciousness the world we want to see. Spend more time there and less time worried about all the things you cannot control. Through your intentional and conscious mind you will, you are changing the world for the better.

56

Divine One, the time has come for you to step into the fullness of your being. To shed the last layers of illusion, to open your all knowing eye and see the truths of this world and the world that will be. We have been preparing you for this moment your entire life and the time has come to utilize your gifts, strengths, and abilities to their fullest potential. The time is now to act, to speak and to move forward in your knowing. To spread the message of truth, and hope, and the new world. We love you Divine One and we are always protecting you, constantly moving you into the right position, and always supporting your highest good. We ask you now to move forward in faith, to cast aside your fears and doubts and BE THE CHANGE you wish to see.

57

Divine One, let yourSelf rest today. Without rest and rejuvenation the spirit feels cramped, not able to fully utilize the wholeness of it's vessel, not able to utilize the clarity of your mind, not able to fully connect in sacred and conscious connection. Rest is one of the most important parts of this life, without it all that you DO and LEARN does not have the chance to integrate into the system. Without rest your nervous system gets run down and burnt out, without rest you can't stand fully in your strength and power. When you rest it's important to give yourSelf complete permission to just be, it's a rest of the body, mind, and spirit, so there should be no judgments or fears of missing out, simply resting knowing the Universe is working FOR YOU as you show up for all parts of yourSelf. So we ask you today to simply be, clear your schedule, find your inner joy and peace, and let that lead you into complete restoration.

58

Divine One, we desire to give you the world, we desire to open you up to all that you are and all that you could be. We desire for you to see yourSelf through our unconditionally loving eyes, to know your worth, to know your strength, to know your divinity and magic. Divine One, you are a sacred presence. You are sacred in all you do and all you are and there is no prerequisite for our love, no prerequisite for our blessing, no prerequisite for miracles to occur. We simply ask that you allow yourSelf to receive, to open, to be with the oneness of this beautiful life knowing that each and every moment, yes even the hard ones, are sacred, that each and every experience is a gift from us to you and that through each moment, each interaction, each shared grace you are healing the world. that as you give to another you give back to yourself, as you forgive another you forgive yourself, and as you walk this earth in bliss you spread magic everywhere you go. We love you Divine One, keep going.

59

Divine One, breathe and know all is well. It's time for you to rest. Not too long in the future great strength, determination, and action will be needed. Very soon you will be asked to step fully into your power, into your leadership, into your calling. You will be asked to lead the masses deeper into awakening, to be a beacon of light in the new world and it will take all the energy, mental discipline and open heartedness you have within you. As we shift into the new way of being there is much work to be done. Now is the time to rest, recharge, get your affairs in order, take an inventory of your life, noticing who and what is no longer serving you. This goes for relationships, thought patterns, habits, ways of living, being and thinking. What in the external world is distracting you from your greater purpose, what pulls you out of your consciousness and peace, and where have you lost discipline and consistency in your conscious ,mindfulness practices? You have this time now to dedicate yourSelf to fully optimizing your body, mind and spirit. So breathe, chill, and keep your heart open. As you serve more you must fill yourself more. We love you. Patience and rejuvenation are key.

60

Divine One, now is the time to RISE in faith. You have been called as a leader of light and truth in this New Earth. You have been called as a Divine Sovereign being to walk in your Highest Timeline here on Earth. To honor your mind, body and spirit as you come into alignment with all that you are. It is your time to experience the joys and wonders of life on Earth in your current lived experience. It is time for you to fully honor and act in accordance with Divine Will. To trust the ways life is happening for you and respond with an open heart and clear mind. This is a call to deepen into Self, to go inward in quiet meditation, to eat and drink pure foods and waters, to detox your life of all energies that would hold you back or siphon your energy. Now is the time to ground into all that you are as you align with your cosmic nature and create Heaven on Earth.

61

Divine One, remember the power of your light, the power of your love, the way your breath aligns you with the Universe and your beliefs create worlds.

You are a powerful co-creator with this Universe, a cherished being of the highest frequencies and as you have this human experience you have everything you need within.

Simply ask for what you want, and then let yourSelf have it. Open yourSelf to the Miracles available to you, know without a doubt that you are worthy here and now and as we come together as a collective we Become the change we seek as we create the New Earth.

62.

Divine One, quiet your mind and know that I am and always will create miracles on your behalf.
It is only your faith that is required.
Faith in the seemingly impossible.
Faith in your ability to receive.
Faith in good things happening for/through you.
When you have faith, you have everything.
And it is in both the good times and the hard ones that faith deepens, that your inner knowing will show you how I am working on your behalf.
And together with your aligned action and loving heart we can do anything.
Breathe into that truth, deepen your faith and as you ask for what you need, move forward knowing that it is already yours.

63

Divine One, you are safe; here, now, in my loving embrace. Your life is unfolding in perfect timing. Each and every lesson you have learned, each obstacle you have overcome has been positioning you and preparing you for what is to come.
Your heart has been expanded to hold all the blessings and miracles waiting for you now.
This is the time to increase your faith, to trust in Divine Timing and know that in the end and in the always- life is happening for you, for the greater good of your heart and soul, for the great good of humanity as a whole.
This human experience is not an easy one but you have done so well navigating through the ebbs and flows. Celebrate yourself. Let yourself rest in my arms, let yourself sink into the love and safety available to you now and always, and know that as you align with the desires of your heart they will be manifest in your waking reality.

64

Divine Collective, humanity is shifting, everything will be brand new. The highest frequency of light is purging the ways of the old, Now is the time to hold steady. To continue to care for your body, mind and spirit, to transmute the energies that do not serve you, to cleanse your food, water, and environment of anything that does not serve your highest good, to align with the highest form of truth and keep your heart and mind in sync. This is the time to breathe deep, stay grounded, and nurture your vessels and we prepare for the new way. This is the time to go within and find safety in the Source energy that is within and all around you. This is the time to stay true to your authentic Self. You are one of many guiding the world into the new earth.

65

Divine One, the infinite knowledge of the Universe lies within you. You are the oracle, the way, the source of the channel, you are it all. You do not need to look outside of yourSelf for the answers you seek, you do not need to do anything to become worthy of accessing this knowledge. For it is what you are. The more aligned with your heart and truth you become the easier it get to access this wisdom, the more in-tune and open to your higher conscious wisdom you are the easier it becomes to interpret the information available to you in all moments. And the more your act from Divine Will the easier it gets to create the reality of your dreams. You are more powerful than you know Divine One and you are never alone in your attempts to access your innate abilities and wisdom. Ask and you shall receive, for it is law.

66

Divine One, I know that sometimes this human existence can feel hard, I know that the doubts, the fears, the limiting beliefs of the ego sometimes feel real and true.
But Divine One, I want you to know that in each and every moment you are held, you are safe, you are in your perfect timeline.
Your life is not something to solve, it's not one big achievement, it's meant to be experiences, lived, moment by moment.
One of the great human traps is the story of the mind, but that was never the mind's purpose.
The mind was meant to work with your heart, to allow you to navigate through life on Earth with ease, using your heart's wisdom to then create words, aligned action, and move from Divine Will.
The mind was meant to help you interact with others and assist your body in all its functions. Your mind was never meant to be the one in control or possess the wisdom, that dear one comes from your heart and the inner knowing of your Soul.
Today I ask you to breathe, to live from that inner knowing, to trust your soul's guidance and follow the call of your heart.
Quiet your mind and be in each moment fully. See where life takes you.
What have you got to lose?

67

Divine One, the idea of surrender might still feel foreign to you. Even if you claim to have done it a million times I ask you this, "Have you ever truly let go? Have you been carried by the sails of the Universe never fearing or wondering for the deepest desires of your heart? But instead knowing with assuredness they are already yours?"

It's not an easy feat living in a state of oneness with all that you are, but it IS your divine mission here on earth to find that feeling of oneness, to pour love into yourSelf and to experience all you can dream.

Start to notice where you still "struggle" where you still fight or resist the ebbs and flows of life. Where those deeply rooted thoughts still creep in, to dissuade you from your full power and ability.

Breathe and know that all is well. Breathe into your doubts and teach them a new way. When you deepen into all that you are and expand fully across the cosmos you will find the bliss you seek. For it is available to you now, you do need to choose it though, to see it though, to believe it.

68

Divine One, I want you to know, you are never truly separate from me, from the Universal Loving Source. You are an extension of me dear one, a piece of my heart resides in yours and a piece of yours in mine. We share breath, we share life. As you grieve I experience grief, as you feel pleasure I experience pleasure. Each and every emotion and experience allows us all to evolve in the One Consciousness Mind we share. All of it is good and perfect. All of it is just as it is, nothing more, nothing less. So breathe sweet one, there is no need to try so hard, no need to attempt to please others, focus on the present moment, experience life fully, the way only you know how and know that that is more than enough.

69

I want you to know from the bottom of my heart that I believe in you.
I see you, doing the work. Waking up every day and creating momentum (even if that just means remembering to breathe)
I see you finding yourself and making those hard but life changing decisions.
I see you trying your best to simply be. Don't give up.
It's all going to be worth it. Just keep breathing and know you are held.

70

Divine One, as you move with the currents of life, as you let your human essence fully come alive you are creating new ripples of life force and energy and experiences for the consciousness of all. We are all connected, all here on this Earth having these experiences in physical form, experiences only ever dreamed of in other dimensions, even the ones that seem hard and uncomfortable. In every moment you are allowing Universal Consciousness to experience new life, to grow, evolve, and expand until the day each and every being returns to that state of Oneness. You can take the pressure off, follow your heart, live moment to moment and know that your living and breathing create new worlds.

71

Hey there, Grief, my old friend. It's been a minute since we've danced together.
I almost forgot the way in which your waves crash into my essence, how I must swim with you rather than resist you.
And so…
I welcome you with open arms; move through me, expand and stretch my heart in ways I didn't know was possible.
Teach me just how deep and true our connection is as I feel into the consciousness of their presence with me now, though they no longer inhabits their physical vessel.
Remind me of just how big their presence in my life and on this Earth was. Remind me of each moment we shared, each word uttered, every hug and kiss exchanged.
Amplify my Love for them, for my family, for mySelf.
Dear Grief, let's move in harmony, breathing into the uncomfortable sensations and knowing that too is Love.
I know that the burn in my heart and the ache in my bones is your way of calling me home, into Love, Remembrance and Grace.
May my breathe deepen, my heart soften, and my Soul awaken with each moment spent in your embrace.

72.

Divine One, where and how you are in this moment, here, now, is perfect. Breathe into the knowing that you can't mess up what is meant for you. You are being positioned and prepared for your next highest timeline. The lessons you are learning now, the way life is happening for you is all for the greater good. You may not see it now but one day you will look back on this time in gratitude and understanding that you were being led, held, and guided every single step of the way. So sink into the here and now, open yourSelf up to learn from life and trust that it's all unfolding in alignment with your Divine Will.

73

Divine One, you are a walking and talking miracle. From your head to your toes and your soul to your bones you are an absolute masterpiece. When external circumstances and experiences aren't going the way your mind and ego might desire them to, it's easy to forget how magical this existence really is. When you can take a step back and zoom out you will see that this moment right here and right now doesn't have to be that serious, it can be approached with lighthearted joy, excitement, the desire to learn. It's only when you become attached to certain outcomes and ways of being that suffering is created. The mere fact that you can breathe, that your heart can beat, that you exist is proof enough of the miracles the Universe creates through you. Remember that and move forward with the knowledge that whatever you are facing can and will be transformed into magic, and in this moment it's exactly what you "need".

74

Divine One, what if I told you that you were enough all by yourself. That you did not require the energy of another to fulfill or sustain you. That you do not require the wisdom, praise, or validation from the outside world to feel worthy. What if that could all come from within?

I promise you it can. It's just that most of the time we won't give ourselves the time and space required to reprogram our nervous system and energy bodies enough to be able to sit with the fullness of ourselves.

We have been taught for so long to bring the external into ourselves and project ourselves onto it. When we take away that structure, all that stuffing and those energy fillers it can feel a bit scary, the hollowness and spaciousness, the depths, and limitless within.

We can panic at the thought of managing that much energy and power and so
we give ourselves away, we avoid and distract and fill back up all the spaces with all the parts of the world that simply are not ours. And we get lost in the sea of otherness. Thinking we require the outer to fulfill the inner.

And a powerful one, it's a lie.

You are capable of managing all that powerful energy. You are deserving of pouring that limitless potential and passion into yourself. You are an infinite vessel and enough in all ways. No matter what.

You are enough.Now. Always. Forever.

75

Divine One, this is the time to keep your frequency high.
To breathe into your knowing and ground into your truth.
It is Time to stand fully in your power and purpose.
Do not be swayed by the low vibrational energies that will continue to come forward by the world as this powerful transition takes place.
It is in your rising, in your steady flow, in your dedication to truth that you will model the new way for the world, it is in your commitment to holding the light that we will transcend the dark energies present on the earth and alchemize that energy to create anew.
You are ready for this, anchor into your Divinity and stand tall knowing the time has come for you to radiate the high vibrational essence of your Soul.

76

Divine One, even in the moments when you don't feel connected, when you get lost in the mind and the ways of the world… You are still held in Love. You can never truly become separate from Source because YOU are an extension of Source. Your connection comes when you clear the mind and drop into the heart, when you allow yourSelf to walk in the God Frequency and reside in Love. And even when you choose to escape, when you choose to misalign, when you choose to forget your essence, you are still deeply connected to it all. And that also means that at anytime you can choose to become conscious of your state of being and choose one more in alignment. Whatever you choose, know that it is perfect and right for you in that moment. It is then you drop the projections and judgements and come into ease.

77

Divine One, you are more loved and supported that you may know.

One day you are going to look back at this time and you are going to be in awe and wonder of yourSelf and the Miracles created by and for you.

Now is the time for faith, for trust, to follow the bliss and allow Life to happen for you and through you.

This is the time to honor, love, and see yourSelf as the cosmic masterpiece you are.

Breathe deep and know everything is about to change.

78

Divine One, your grief is simply proof of the loss you are perceiving. It's proof of the love shared, the appreciation, the gratitude, the special place in your heart the person or experience held. Your grief is a powerful emotion, not something to run from or get over but rather something to embrace, to honor, to open to. Your grief will expand your heart and soul, it will show you the depths of your Love and if you allow it to, your grief will show you that you haven't really lost at All. Because Divine One, you are connected to the whole of the Universe, while your physical vessel may be run by time, the who that you really are is immortal, Universal Consciousness never dies, never leaves, only Evolves into the greater whole. So breathe, grieve, and know that through it all you are loved.

79

Divine One, we wish to remind you of the immortal nature of your being. To remind you that you are infinitely held, loved and connected to the Universal I AM... That you are the powerful Consciousness currently embodied in human form and that through that knowing you are never alone.

80

Divine One, Life is your playground.
Each experience and sensation whether you deem is "good" or "bad" is an opportunity for Source Consciousness to expand through human experience.
You are an extension of Source Consciousness and everything you encounter activates different parts of your individual consciousness and ripples into the collective.
We are all constantly evolving and expanding the One True Self.
Allow yourSelf to see Life as your playground, experiment with interactions and sensations.
Let your mind be free of judgments and attachments, let your heart be open and welcoming.
And watch as even the hardest moments become miraculous opportunities to expand.

81

Divine One, breathe and know all is well. Breathe into the depths of your being and into your highest heights and know that you are loved, held and supported in all that you do. Whether you desire rest and isolation and are filled with energy and desire to be out in the world, know that what is here now is perfect. Don't allow your thoughts to persuade you from what you feel in your soul and remember as you speak your truth and follow your heart you can never truly fail. Pay no attention to the perceptions of others as you align with Truth but rather let their judgements or wonderings also be perfect. As you turn within and commit to what is in alignment for You, miracles will unfold endlessly and this life will become an incredible experience of evolution and growth.

82

Divine One, Life is your teacher and Love is your classroom.
It's through your relationships, interactions, and experiences with others that ultimately define your life and reality.
The way you perceive yourSelf based on the perceptions of others, the way you perceive the world based on your interactions with others.
It's all connected.
Each experience woven together with the thought patterns, beliefs, and ideas in your mind create your reality.
That is why self-reflection and awareness of your core beliefs is so important.
That's why doing the work to unplug from the eternal and choose from your heart allows you to shift realities.
As you step back and simply observe, as you go within and answer the call of your Soul you will see the truth.
And from that truth you discover absolute freedom, existential bliss, Embodied Divinity.

83

Divine One, miracles are available to you in each moment of each day. As you step back from the circumstances of life and truth within to the cosmic masterpiece at your core you will find great power to alchemize and transmute whatever you might be feeling into whatever you desire. You are worthy of miracles now, you are connected to Oneness Now, you are whole and perfect as you are… It's in coming into alignment with your heart and clear mind that you will find ease and grace lace your existence and life will become your playground.

84

Divine One, the time is upon us, as a collective we must rise in Love. To harness our strength and walk in faith each day. It is through our collective vibrational shifts we will pave the way, as each individual awakens we come together as one and stand as Divine Witness, Leaders, Way Showers of what is to come. A world of peace, love and harmony can and will exist, it is our job to create it. It's getting easier and easier to see through the illusions of the world, to make your own way, and create communities and lifestyles more in alignment with truth and love. Continue to turn within, to seek the all knowing guidance within you, and be brave enough to do things your way.

85

Divine One, you need not try to connect with higher realms, you need not try to vibrate higher, you need not try to shift.
These things happen naturally as you tune into your heart, as you align with the Divinity at the core of who you are.
You are always connected, always vibrating at the perfect rhythm and always able to deepen that connection as you sync your breath and heart with the present moment.
In your everyday moments you are connected to Source, In your deepest meditations you are connected to source, in your laughter and your tears you are connected to Source because Divine One you yourSelf are the embodiment of Source in human form, an extension of that high vibrational, all knowing energy, it's what you are.
As you acknowledge that and live from the heart you will understand that separation is impossible and in each moment and breath you are connected, held, and rising in your own Divinity.

86

Divine One, who you are is enough. Breathe and now you are in your perfect timeline. Where you are right here, right now is preparing you for all that is to come. Be present with who you are in this moment; loving and accepting of all the ways you show up and all the ways you do not. It is in your honoring of who you are here and now that you evolve into who you will become. The answers you seek are within you, they do not lie with some external source or power but within the essence of your being. At the core of your being you are already whole, already living at your highest, already enlightened, ascended and awakened. As you shed the layers of disbelief and doubt you will see more clearly the elevated state of being within. As you live from there you exude joy and create miracles. And it all starts within being here, now. Loving whatever is.

87

Divine One, this life on Earth is all about the lens from which you are viewing it. You can choose to view this world and its experience with disdain and anger, obstacles, and unfairness. You can choose to view this worldly experience through a lens of love and joy, synchronicity and magic. And whatever lens you see it through affects the way you feel about it and your day to day experiences with life. Your lens can sometimes be affected by your trauma, your past, your shadows, and your wounds and it is up to you to consciously clean up the lens and create a different view. As you look in the mirror and become really honest with the images you are projecting onto the world you discover great power in your ability to change them. So today I ask you this... Can you view the world through a different lens? If only for a moment and see what changes?

Divine One, that call to rest you feel is also a call to release and integrate. We are shifting at a rapid rate and with the coming of fall it will only accelerate. Your body is releasing all the old stories, programs and patterns and they need to be felt, processed and released as you move forward on your journey. This is a call to take time to both rest and reflect. To process the past, learn, evolve and grow. Whether you process through journaling, meditation, or healing sessions with others carve out time to do so now. We are in the final stretch and the energies are only growing more intense from here. The lighter your energy field the easier the transition will be. Listen to your body, witness what is revealing itself and take aligned action in the direction of your soul. You've got this. And you are never truly alone.

88

Sweet, Divine, Soul- thank you for being here on Earth at this time. Thank you for your courage, your love, your presence, your beingness. Your choice to be here, to be a part of this massive shift in humanity, your desire to create more magic and wonder in this lifetime is awe inspiring. And we want you to know that your actions, your desires, your intentions, and your heart do not go unnoticed. We see you, we witness your innate goodness, we feel the pure intentions of your heart, and we understand the longing of your soul to simply "be home" and Divine One, please know this, your actions here and now in this lifetime are creating a ripple across all lifetimes, creating grace, compassion and miracles for your simultaneous Selves in others dimensions and this one here, now. Every moment you are shifting closer and closer to the vibrational state of the New Earth. Feel our love, our gratitude, and praise for you and keep going. You're doing a great job.

89

Divine One, breathe, we know you don't "want:" to rest right now, we know you feel you are doing something wrong, not doing enough, not being enough. But dear one, who and how you are is perfect and you are living in your Divine Timeline. A change is coming, all your needs physical, financial, spiritual, mental and emotional are being met and will continue to be met, look back at the evidence and have faith in this here and now. Sink into your heart space, into the present moment and surrender, rest and Be at ease. We are preparing you for what is to come and while it will all be good you will need strength, fortitude and energy. Keep the faith, believe our words and embody your highest divinity as you sink into the here and now. We love you and we are always here whether or not you feel us.

90

Divine One, you are embarking on one of the most powerful times of your current existence; a time of great change, of great growth and unheard of Evolution. A revolution of the heart and soul as light workers, heart centered leaders, mystics, and like minds come together as One to create a shift in the collective that will change the Earth as we know it forevermore. There is a reason for the call in your soul, a reason for the softening, a reason for the foresight, each moment of your life thus far has been preparing and positioning you for the HERE and NOW. There is no need to fear, no need for urgency, it is all unfolding in perfect time, the only thing to DO is to BE, in alignment with your heart, your soul, your breath, the present moment. As you sink into your Beingness all will be revealed. It's time to trust, to surrender, to sink into the unknown and affirm that you are safe, held and supported.

91

Divine One, remember that alignment with your breath is alignment with the Universe. As you slow and deepen your breath you come into full alignment with the Here and Now, the power of the Present and the One Truth. As you find harmony with your breath you find harmony with your inner beingness, your divinity, your light. As you consciously breathe you consciously expand. You will witness your worries, doubts and fears dissolve, replaced by peace, ease, and fulfillment. Your breath is the most powerful tool you've been given in this lifetime. Return to it often and fan the eternal flame.

92

Divine One, you are loved endlessly, you are never truly alone when you stay open to and aware of the Source within and around you.
In fact, nothing can separate you from Source, you only create the illusion of separation with your own mind, with your feelings of unworthiness and not enoughness ,
but Divine One, those beliefs are untrue. You are worthy, good, perfectly enough right here and right now.
As you lean into the truth of all that you are you will feel that powerful connection with Source and you will know just how special you are.
As you embrace your Universal Support you will stand taller, speak with more fervor, love deeper and welcome in all that is meant for you with open and deserving arms.
So breathe Divine One, feel Source within and all around you and know that you are LOVE.

93

Divine One, the world is changing, the time of the great revolution is among us. A large number of you now see through the illusion, you see the way you've been divided, manipulated, oppressed, and contained and so many are rising up and fighting back. Now more than ever it is important to remember that the power lies in alignment and there are now more aligned with truth on this Earth than there are those blind. Continue to follow the truth of your heart, to create the communities, systems, and information required for the New Earth to thrive. Be mindful of what you hear and see on mainstream news and social media and when in doubt turn within. You are about to witness a massive purge of distortion and untruth as more and more awaken. There is a reason you chose to be alive here and now, remember that and move forward with your heart open and mind clear.

94

Divine One, you are braver than you know, stronger than you might currently feel, more capable than you realize.

This time on Earth has not been easy, you have moved through many obstacles, times of upheaval, fear, and thwarted attempts of external control.

You have played your part in the current revolution and you continue to rise again and again.

It's important that you remember your sovereignty at this time, that you never have to comply with the desires of outside forces and you will always know what is in alignment with your soul's truth as you turn within.

Stand tall and continue to choose the path of freedom and sovereignty as the world begins to shift. We need all the leaders of light and truth that we can get.

95

Divine One, imagine if you loved yourself even a shred of the amount you loved them.
If you showed up for your dreams the way you so gallantly showed up for theirs?
What if you invested the amount of energy into your own soul's creation that you did on fixing the problems or needs of another.
What if even for a moment you brought it all back to YOU.
Would you tremble in fear of the love you longed for?
Would you receive and fill with open arms?
Would it give you the life force energy you've needed to finally do the damn thing?
It's not for me to say. But I do ask… Can you go within? Ask these questions… sit with the truth. And then
Align and Act.

96

Divine One, it's possible to be kind & have strong and solid boundaries. Sometimes setting boundaries is the most loving thing you can do. Don't let the world convince you that saying what you need & honoring yourself is mean/selfish. You get to come first and THEN you will easily step into full presence with others.

97

You always have a choice and there are unlimited possibilities on what to choose so make sure you're choosing was in alignment with your heart and soul and not someone else's dream for you

98

Divine One, we aren't meant to live in a state of suffering. In fact, if there are moments that you are not feeling peace, joy, and ease it is your sure sign that there is something out of alignment in your field. Note, there is nothing wrong or bad about these emotions, they are simply asking you to return to love for what is here now rather than resist it. It's a powerful concept to live by; allowing your internal navigation system to guide you into a state of harmony and alignment. When you can listen to your body and allow it to bring you back in tune with the desires of your heart. When you can listen to the anxiety, the anger, the energies that come alive within you and simply open your heart further as you sense what it is you truly desire in each moment. You find clarity, knowing and direction. Learn to listen to what your body and emotions are telling you, letting them lead you back to peace and grace.

99

Divine One, The Universe is alive within you. Your essence is a gift to this world as Source energy experiences life through you. Each individual being is an extension of Source energy, having their own human experience and allowing the Whole (Oneness of the Universe) to collectively experience each and every aspect of life on Earth. With each experience, sensation, knowing, and feeling you are allowing the Universal Consciousness from which we are all connected, alive in, part of to experience it too. As each and every being on Earth allows themSelves to come into full acceptance of this knowing and operate from both the individual and the Whole, all of humanity will shift into the next paradigm of living, called the New Earth. The New Earth is being created now in this timeline and many are experiencing the effects of that great shift in their day to day energetic experience of Being. As more and more open to all that they are, more and more are awakened, a constant domino effect of shifts in consciousness. One by One we are transitioning into the New Earth.

100

Divine One, breathe, slow and steady. You are more powerful than you know, more wise than you know, more beautiful than you know. You are a perfect creation, a human image yes, but eternal soul, clear and pure consciousness, the frequency of Divine love is what you're made of. The radiating light within you, the spark behind your eye, the glimmer of excitement within your heart… that is your truth. You are never left alone, but rather always fully tapped into the cosmic rays of the ethers. And they guide you closer and closer to yourself if you would just listen. Be with yourself and all that you are and let the things of the world fall away. Held in grace now and forever, you are the one you have been waiting for.

101

I am not defined by my praises or criticism. I am not defined by the love that echos through me or the rage that boils within. I am not defined by my faults or my achievements. I am not defined by my beauty or my imperfections. All of it is simply me. And all of it is worthy.

Sometimes I fall apart… *I am still worthy.*
Sometimes everything goes my way… *I am still worthy.*
Sometimes I react from my trigger… *I am still worthy.*
I have hurt others…*I am still worthy.*
I have been hurt…*I am still worthy.*
I am a cosmic masterpiece …*I am still worthy.*
I embrace and fully embody my humanity …*I am still worthy.*
I have stretch marks and extra fat…*I am still worthy.*
I'm am strong and toned…*I am still worthy.*
I curse frequently…*I am still worthy.*
I love with all my heart…*I am still worthy.*
I have boundaries like a mutha f*cker…*I am still worthy.*
I lead with a wide open heart …*I am still worthy.*
I have judged others and myself …*I am still worthy.*
I have compassion and grace…*I am still worthy.*
I have told lies that hurt others…*I am still worthy.*
I have told truths that caused others pain…*I am still worthy.*

I have triggered and been triggered…*I am still worthy.*

I love to be f*cked…*I am still worthy.*

I love to make love…*I am still worthy.*

I have suffered…*I am still worthy.*

I have failed…*I am still worthy.*

I have won…*I am still worthy.*

I have achieved…*I am still worthy.*

I have experienced true bliss…*I am still worthy.*

I have experienced maddening depression…*I am still worthy.*

I have worn guilt like a blanket…*I am still worthy.*

I have have abused my body and mind…*I am still worthy.*

I have healed my body and found forgiveness for myself…*I am still worthy.*

I am worthy here. now. With it all.

And so are you!

(Drop your own truths below)

I_____……And I am still worthy!

102

Divine One, you are a powerful creator of both this world and the next, as you choose to create consciously in both the inner and outer realm you will begin to see your desires take shape. Breathing deep into your own essence what do you feel? What do you see? Do you see the magic? The power? The light?
Do you see the ways you can create miracles by simply seeing them in your mind's eye and believing them fully in your heart? This life is a gift whether you choose to see it that way or not, it is a gift to your inner essence, your soul, your Source, and it's through those eyes that you witness the magnificence of all you are, all we are, as we walk this earth in this lifetime. You don't need to see it to believe it, you just need to feel it within and allow it to happen through you. Your guardians are with you always, your highest self always available to impart wisdom as you allow it. Tune in today, you might like what you see.

103

Divine One, can you open your heart and clear your mind. Witness the grace available to you in all moments as you become deeply present with the here and now.
Can you breathe in life and exhale doubt? I know right now life can feel hard, with all the energetic upgrades, new ways of being and the fear that can often come with stepping away from the status quo.
And Divine One, I also know that you are ready.
You are ready to stand in your power and own your gifts, you are ready to walk in love and choose the path less traveled as we collectively create the new earth.
You are ready to receive all you have been waiting for.
You are ready to have it all.
Let go of the doubt and own your Divine Potential, take action aligned with your Divine Will and stay present with the frequency of love.
As you do this you will begin to experience everlasting peace and joy in each and every moment and circumstance.

104

Divine One, breathe and know you are loved. Divine Grace is all around you, love ripples through you, truth pervades you. You are a powerful Soul, a mighty being with a unique mission here on Earth. As you align with your breath and this present moment you will experience complete clarity. As you sink into clarity and exercise choice based on alignment with Divine Will you will create worlds. Kaleidoscope visions will come to life before you. Your Will and Clarity may invoke resistance in others, but Divine One, their reaction or response to your aligned actions does not diminish, your worthiness, your goodness. For you are Good, and perfect and true as you walk with your highest Self and the opinion of others can never take that away. So breathe, speak, love, and act in accordance with what feels aligned with truth and watch the shackles fall away.

105

Divine One, as you breathe deep into yourself and sink into the rhythm of the Universal Heart you discover a centered and powerful wisdom. Untapped knowledge and energy is available to you in each moment as you find clarity of mind, peace of heart and alignment with the Soul. It is through your breath you expand into Universal Consciousness and break into realities previously unknown. As you consciously breathe, ground, and find your center you align with the frequency of the New Earth and create a ripple of change across the collective by simply existing. As you remember the magic and mastery within you step into the remembering of all that you are and ever were. So breathe deep today, consciously and intentionally align with the powers of breath and in doing so align with the wonders and miracles the Universe has to offer.

106

Divine One, your human vessel is a powerful tool that allows you (consciousness) to live in this waking reality. It is the hard drive to your infinite energy on this earth. Having an intimate and healthy relationship with your human body allows you to experience the fullness of this reality. Your body's intuitive and primal nature holds the answers you seek as you navigate this vast terrain. As you align mind, body, and spirit you experience optimal energy, clear knowing, Divine Will, and the power to manifest and materialize your greatest desires. You've experienced consciousness without a body in many dimensions, that timeless form is your true nature but you came to Earth to master this human experience. To deny your body is to be spiritually homeless in this existence. One of the greatest achievements in this lifetime is to master your physical body and still understand that you are NOT your body but rather the consciousness operating within and around it. You are the one observing, holding the "controller" in your proverbial hands and your body is the avatar roaming the vast landscapes of this projected reality. Remember that and you will find great ease within as you navigate this human experience.

107

Divine One, you have every answer you seek within you. As you tune into your primal nature and follow your gut instincts you will be led in all you do. Society has taken you away from your inner knowing, blasting you with external stimuli and causing you to second guess your instincts. As you ground into the present moment and learn to listen to that inner knowing you will be led into a new reality; one of love, creation and ease. There is a powerful global shift taking place now as old societal structures are crumbling and the way of the New Earth is being created. You play a powerful role in its creation as you learn to harness your inner joy and lead from love. As you see the abundance and blessings all around you and shift your perception of this world you will project a new reality and in doing so raise the frequency of the collective consciousness. The greatest thing you can do right now is deepen your love for yourSelf and Source and ground into what is Here, Now.

108

Divine One, how often do you let your heart lead the way? How often do you open to the beauty and magic in each felt experience? Like the flame of a candle our hearts light dims when closed off from the world, without the breath of life, love, connections stoking its flame it fades and becomes cold. Divine One, your heart is a masterpiece, a powerful tool that guides you deep into yourSelf, into your true nature, and as you lead from that heart-centered knowing you stumble into a world of Oneness, Connection, and Love for ALL. It is from this place you perceive the true beauty and wonder afforded to you in this human existence. In no other dimension do you have a heart like this one, in no other existence do you have the ability to FEEL what you feel here in this human experience. We know how scary it can be sometimes, living in what seems an open and exposed way, but it's' from there the voice of your Soul is amplified, it's from there you break away from the ways of the old and forge paths to the New. It's from there You truly LIVE. So Divine One, we ask for today, can you open your heart to the world, can you let it take the lead and be brave enough to walk into the unknown?

109

Divine One, breathe deep and know you are held. Our love for you is bigger than you could ever imagine. In each moment of each day we are holding you, envisioning you in your essence, your power, in love. We know this human experience has been more confusing than you originally thought it would be. Many souls take for granted the privilege of the all knowing consciousness they have in other realms. The forgetting, the perceived separation you experience here on Earth can be devastating to the human psyche, but your Soul, your essence, your consciousness remembers. Deep inside you know without a doubt that you are ONE with Source, that you are never alone and that you are always held. When your human mind can remember that this experience on Earth changes, you see clearly how life is happening for and through you, you feel supported in each new experience no matter how "negative" the human mind may label it. And Divine One, it is in this knowing and remembering that everything changes, that you become more for you, more of us, more One. It's from this knowing that you become FREE and WHOLE. So wherever you are in this moment, remember the truth of your Soul, zoom out, and SEE that you are exactly where you are meant to be.

110

Divine One, as you align with the frequency of joy and let yourself expand into greater consciousness you gain a clear view of this reality. We want to remind you that your waking reality is a projection of your subconscious mind and at any moment you have the ability to change the images being projected and therefore create a new reality in alignment with your desires. And Divine One, there doesn't have to be a lag in what you desire and what is created. When backed with power and belief, when fully harnessed and a deep knowing is present things can (and often do) change in the blink of an eye. Remember, time and space only exist to the ego so there is no real timeline for how long it must take for your desires to materialize, the longer you can hold the frequency of the new reality, the longer you can walk and live in the belief that it's happening for you the faster it comes. For it is already created and waiting for YOU to receive it. So breathe, know and feel what you desire and sooner than later it will be.

111

Divine One, emotions are powerful tools that you can use to your advantage. Emotions allow you to notice where and how you are in response to the love that is around you. Emotions fuel your body with energy that can be harnessed and alchemized to create anew. Emotions/Energy are a means of guidance, a language between the Divine and Human Mind. It's when you can notice the stories that come with the Emotions/Energy, that you can choose to invest more in such a story or choose one more in alignment with your soul's desires and knowing. Emotional Alchemy is the process of becoming aware of your emotions, noticing the energy you are investing in the stories attached to them, and choosing to invest in more of what you desire as you purify and recycle the energy within your system. You will feel every sensation and when you label it just that, a sensation, and nothing more you can use it accordingly. It's when you create weighty labels that come with stories that the energy creates more of what you do not desire. So today simply start to observe the stories that come with certain emotions and make a choice to invest the energy present into stories that feel and serve the highest good.

112

Divine One, even in the darkest of times there is light. Even in the deepest suffering there can be joy. This human experience is multifaceted, multi sensational, just like you. You came here desiring to experience a vast array of emotions and sensations, a vast array of circumstances and situations. You came here knowing that you were eternal, timeless, limitless. A soul here to experience humanity, in this world but never of this world. It's only in your journey of humanity that you have forgotten the true nature of personal reality. The nature of your being and the vastness of your light. Divine One, when you anchor into what you really are there is no human experience that can rock you, not even death will make you shutter because you see Divine One, you will already know that your essence, your consciousness is immortal and untouchable. So loosen up, let yourself be fully alive here and now and sink into the light so deeply that you consume and embrace each facet of the dark.

113

Divine One, each moment, each experience, each circumstance is a divine one. Each step you take is leading you closer and closer to the fullness of your being. It's in embracing and being fully present in each moment that you experience the fullest life. In knowing that even when it doesn't seem like life is going your way, even when you have no idea how your dreams will become manifest; that you are being divinely held, protected, and positioned for your greatest good. You came here with a soul knowing of this evolution. Your soul chose each person, place and experience knowing that in the end it would benefit your best and highest good. You chose this life and these circumstances with a bigger picture in mind, the evolution of your soul and even the evolution and healing of humanity. Life is unfolding for you in divine timing and in the perfect way and as you can deepen into that knowing you will feel the love and support around you even when it becomes dark. Know this Divine One, you are in the right place and the right time and you can never mess up anything that was meant for you. Your dreams get to come true in the exact right way for you.

114

Divine One, you are the oracle, the all knowing, transformative essence of the Universe, you are the expression of Source/God itSelf. You Divine One, possess the answers you seek, the key to your soul's greatest evolution lies within you. As you integrate your Divinity with your human form you become a vessel of pure, unlimited knowing, seeing the world from a gnostic view, incorporeal, timeless, ever expanding. It's in this way of being that you unlock the fullness of this human experience and see it clearly for what it is, a chance to evolve the consciousness of the Universal Collective. And you Divine One chose to come here to complete this task. It's time to let go of the ways of the world and while it is true you are in it, you must remember you have never been Of it. You are cosmic stardust, you are Source incarnate, you are the epitome of Divinity in Human form. Embrace your wholeness and live accordingly. The time is now.

115

Divine One, this earthly journey is filled with experiences of every kind; it was meant to be. You are here to expand, to experience, to evolve. There is a common misconception that it's meant to be all sunshine and roses, that happiness is the answer and you have to feel good in all moments. That is simply not the case and actually quite counter to everything you signed up for when you made your journey to Earth. You see, Divine One, you came here as a fragment of Source Consciousness under the premise that you would experience a vast array of emotions both "good and bad" both "pleasurable and Painful" both light and dark. You chose this knowing that with each experience you and therefore the wholeness of Source would evolve and expand into deeper depths and great knowing. You came here for the Evolution of the Soul. Your pain, doubts, fears, and darkness are not something to run from or avoid but rather parts of this human experience to be embraced and cherished, and as you do you harness even more life force energy to create more of what you desire. So today we ask you to redefine your views of pain and open to every sensation and experience available to you now. From there you can create your wildest dreams and live a truly free life on Earth.

116

Divine One, big deep breaths and come back to the here and now. You live in a timeless universe with unlimited potential and unmatched possibilities. And we know it isn't always easy to navigate the energies, especially when you have unseen and intergenerational forces still alive within your DNA. And Divine One we want you to know that you have the power here and now to release and transmute any and all energy that isn't yours, to stand fully in your truth and power. And that as you do the inner work to stand in your sovereignty that work is reflected throughout your earth family line. If you are ready to harness all that is yours repeat after me: "For the good of all and the harm of none, I Now call back my power, energy, Will and authority from any and all beings, people, places, timelines, and events taking it from me with or without my consent. I call it back healed, cleansed and operating at the highest frequency of Love. I feel it surging back through me now. I anchor into my truth, my essence, my souls knowing. I stand in light, I stand in love, I stand in truth. Amen" as you feel the surge of energy moving through you allow yourSelf to ground, breathe and be. Repeat as often as necessary. And remember as you focus on standing in your own immaculate energy you heal the world.

117

Divine One, you are more powerful than you know. The reality you see around you now was first formed within your mind, within your beliefs, and each and every choice you have made. Many aspects of your current reality were formed from thought patterns and ideas that didn't truly belong to you or resonate with your soul's truth. These beliefs and ideas came from your external conditioning, from your childhood, from social media and more. There is a powerful energy in the collective bodies of thought and it's easy to be swayed by them. You are being asked now to step away from all groupthink, all bodies of collective being and take time to explore your own inner world and psyche, to discover what truly aligns with you and who you desire to be. What you desire to experience and witness for the remainder of your life on earth. And then fine tune your thought patterns and ways of being to what you truly desire. The first step is becoming the observer of the mind to get a clear view on what stories you have been telling yourself and then begin stepping away from your stories. You have the power to change your entire waking reality Divine One, start here.

118

Divine One, you are the master alchemist, the magician, the evolutionary. You have the ability to harness and alchemize all the energy before you into something truly great. And as you make yourSelf your first priority and truly take the steps to ground, hydrate and clear your field you will find yourSelf in alignment with your highest and best timeline. There is great potential in the energy present here and now, the ability to truly see beyond worlds and release all that is binding you to the past ways of being. As you choose to move forward in integrity with yourSelf, your truth, and your soul's essence you plant seeds of months and years to come and soon will reap the rewards of all you've rooted into here and now. You divine one, have the power to transmute any energy and become the true master of your life. As you deepen into that knowing and move forward with a deep faith that it is all working out for you in the perfect way and the perfect time you will experience deep and foundational peace as you create and open to all that is to come.

119

Divine One, the Universe wants you to experience joy, pleasure and ease. You are meant to feel magic and wonder and sink into infinite abundance. These things are a natural part of who you are. Your divinity is in complete alignment with ease, with wealth, with joy. It is only the thought patterns and beliefs created by the human experience that have clouded your knowing of that. At any moment you can choose to open up to all that is meant for you and more. In any moment you can choose to shed the shoulds, the woulds, the expectations, the judgements, the fears and doubts and instead open to possibilities and magic. When you allow yourself to relax, to trust and surrender to life happening for you now you will experience countless miracles. When you drop the hustle and the need to achieve you will access infinite inspiration and passion that will lead you to the life of your wildest dreams. As your Inner Divine Masculine and Feminine learn to dance together you will open your eyes to a world of abundance in every direction. So breathe, be, and let yourSelf receive.

120

Divine One, if you are having trouble manifesting the desires of your heart or if your dreams feel just out of reach the solution is simple. Go within. You see your inner reality forms your external one and while your heart might desire one thing on a soul level if your mind and ego are operating from internal beliefs that differ there will always be a gap. In order to align your body, mind, and spirit and truly create and manifest with ease you must start with your core internal beliefs. You discover those by observing your external reality, by noticing your thoughts and fears, your doubts, and resistance. It's by telling yourself the truth about the beliefs you are rooted into that you can clearly see where the gap occurs. With that valuable information you can adopt new beliefs that match your desired outcome. This is a powerful thing, you are a powerful being.

121

Divine One, you have the ability in each and every moment to choose a better feeling thought, a higher vibrational state, to step into the frequency of love. Directing the focus on your conscious mind and taking reign over your ego will allow you to become the master of your life and create the reality you desire. It is only when we get lost in the past or projected into the future that we miss out on the infinite power and potential that the present moment holds. Here and NOW you have everything you need to create a massive shift. So breathe deep into this moment, focus on what you desire, let it take roots within you as you sink into gratitude for it all and live each moment as if it were already happening. That is the secret to a prosperous life.

122

Divine One, it is in coming together as a collective with one common goal, to return to Love, that you will change the entire world. For the past few decades more and more light workers have awakened and the last few years we have seen the masses awaken. Up until now each light worker has worked individually to raise their frequency and step into remembrance of all that they are and now is the time to come together. It is in unity, collaboration and connection that you will change the frequency of the world and create the New Earth. Through each individual's tools, gifts, talents and knowings you have each piece of the collective puzzle. As you come together to unite the whole, great change will take place on your planet for the better. You are watching in "real-time" as the old is being swept away and all falsities are crumbling. What will be left is a blank slate for you to collectively rise together and create the world you always dreamed of. A world of peace, community, equality and love. So we ask you to RISE in LOVE and JOIN the rEVOLution.

123.

Divine One, you are the light of the world. Light force energy is what you are made of, the pure frequency of love. It is that energy that created you and that energy that resides within you here and now. YOU ARE the light. And so if in this moment the world seems dark, shine brighter, anchor in and let yourself be transformed by that which you are made of. Anchor into love, into truth, into being and know that you are being Divinely held and protected through it all. Choosing to be a light worker, choosing to forge a new path as we collectively create the new Earth is no easy task. And yet you did choose it and you are doing it. You are creating deep and permeating change within yourself and therefore the world. You are making a difference and you are amplifying the goodness present here on Earth now. To continue to flow with the elements and stay grounded in your light; self-care, energetic hygiene and an abundance of grace and compassion are necessary. Allow yourself to simply be and let the light do its magic as it works through you.

124.

Divine One, you always have a choice. You have a choice in how you respond to the ways life is happening for you. You have a choice in how you perceive your circumstance. You have a choice in how you respond to your feelings. You have a choice in all that you do. And we understand that at times that might feel overwhelming, but it doesn't have to be. As you surrender to the present moment, to what is happening here and now and simply breathe into it all, into yourSelf you will see that it's all simply a projection of the deepest parts of your psyche. That as you step into your Divinity and Oneness with all that is the fear falls away and a deep sense of empowerment takes over as you realize you are always safe. You don't have to make your circumstance or feelings mean anything more than they are, simply something you are experiencing now that will shift later. You have the power to consciously choose each next step, do so from the safety of the present moment and the Way will be shown to you.

125.

Divine One, can you accept what is? Can you accept what is here and now? What you are feeling, experiencing, opening to? It's all perfect, all for your highest good, all Divine. We know that it is tempting to call the lighter feelings good and the heavier feeling bad, but Divine One, all emotions, all feelings, all circumstances are simply tools on your path to your highest spiritual understanding and greatest good.

126.

Divine One your emotions are powerful tools to steer your clearly back to love, back to truth, back to oneness. It's when we drop our judgments and labels and simply allow ourSelves to experience life to its fullest potential that we find ourSelves truly FREE. So breathe and let what is, BE. There is nothing to fix, nothing to alter, nothing to control. When you walk into it all with wonder you will find that life is full of wonder and therefore, wonderful.

127.

Divine One, we want to remind you of the sacred connection between YOU (the observer) and your physical vessel. Your body, your human form, your physical nature is a gift to be cherished in this lifetime. To be disconnected from your body is to be spiritually homeless.. You are quite literally HERE on EARTH to have the human experience and that is simply not possible without a connection to and understanding of the sacred nature of your corporeal form. We ask you to reconnect with this sacred part of you, to care for it with the utmost respect, to nourish it, love it, honor it and form a bond with it so that you might find the deepest sense of meaning, connection and exaltation in this unique form. Remember Divine One, the human experience is one of the few conscious existences with so many sensory experiences, so many felt emotions and sensations. Let yourSelf experience it all to the FULLEST and you will discover a whole new world and a purely magical way of being.

128.

Divine One, at this time we ask you to trust that life is happening for you, that whatever is, is good, is love, is truth. That as you sink into that knowing and dance through life's unfolding without grasping for control you will be led into the most magical place. A place of freedom, of beauty, of uninhibited love. It is in your Divine Surrender that you deepen into your own embodied divinity, that you have the ability to create worlds, to live out your dreams, and walk through this life with deep trust and peace. Divine One, we ask you to sink into the knowing that in each and every experience, even the ones that feel hard, you are being protected and positioned for your greatest good. It is in knowing that you will be set free from the shackles of control and able to stand in love and alignment with all. Go within, find your truth, and radiate love for the world to see. This is how you set yourSelf free.

129.

Divine One, you are everything and you are nothing. The embodiment of the highest level of consciousness in walking, talking form. Your vessel is a sacred home for your soul. Life on Earth; your master teacher. It is in each and every human experience that you expand into the truth of all that you are. Your form is a tool that higher consciousness (the real you) uses to learn, to grow, to experience new dimensions, thought forms, sensations and knowings. This life is an opportunity to expand into oneness with it all as you afford yourSelf the opportunity to make the most of this wild adventure called life. To see each moment in great reverence, to treat each connection and object as a sacred masterpiece and to hold yourself and others in the frequency of life. This life experience is your greatest gift and teacher in this incarnation, it's up to you to heed the call.

130.

Divine One, the truth will set you free. The truth is the way. What is here now is truth. As you use your words, energy and vibration to align with the truth you will experience everlasting freedom and ease. As you come into alignment with life unfolding, see the present moment as the deeply loving expression of truth you will no longer feel the need to argue with life, you will no longer need to resist. And as you step into flow you will see that life is always happening for you. As you use your words to clearly express your needs, desires, thoughts and feelings without the need to manipulate or hold back in order to protect another you will find yourself experiencing deep peace, and while the truth may activate those misaligned it is all done in the frequency of love. When you are aligned with what is true dear one, you become truth itself and in that moment you are free. In that moment you are One.

131.

Divine One, sound and vibration is the language of the Soul. It's through your voice, your vibration, and your resonance that you attract similar vibrations. As you align with the truth of your Soul, as you align with life unfolding, as you align with the Way being shown to you, you will begin to resonate more and more with higher levels of consciousness and higher vibration things and being. When you step out of alignment or truth there is a dissonance within your field of consciousness. This dissonance repels the desires of your soul. Through conscious breath, aligned action, and good feeling thoughts you will begin to transform your physical reality and shift timelines. The more in alignment you become the easier this life is to navigate. You will no longer need to try, you will simply be in and at peace with all around you.

132.

Divine One, love makes the world go around. It is in your love for yourSelf and others that you open to a new world. That you allow your human self and Divine Self to become one and in doing so open to the love, magic and Divine support all around you. Love is meant to feel good, it is unconditional and unwavering and it is only in our judgements toward self and others that we create separation and pain. But Divine One, Love is here now, whatever IS here now, IS Love, it is only your perception of WHAT IS HERE that is creating distortion and separation. In truth, you can never be separate from the Divine Love that YOU are. It simply exists in each moment, each breath, each experience happening here and now. When you truly embrace the truth that life is happening FOR you and all unfolding now is through the flow of Universal Love, as you observe your ego rather than identity with it, you will find a beautiful flow of love within, a powerful stillness in all you do, and harmony in each moment. So breathe into LOVE here and now and see the world through a new lens.

133.

Divine One, you know how to be totally human and you've experienced deep connection with the divinity within, you've soared through the cosmos and roamed the ethers. Now is the time to bring the cosmic into the human, to live in your Divine Knowing, Your Godly Essence, your Cosmic Consciousness while fully embodied in the human. It's allowing your highestSelf to embrace the shadows, the perceived flaws, pains, failures and loving those too. It's about allowing your Divine Self to experience the deepest joy, love, pleasure. It's about experiencing those moments without putting so much thought or weight into it. To honor each and every moment and experience for exactly what it is, an extension of Source itSelf experiencing life on Earth and with each lived experience evolving deeper and deeper into itSelf, into Its OneSelf. So LIVE and do it FULLY, alive in each moment, conscious of your Divinity, fully embracing the human experience. That's how you live life and enjoy it too.

134.

Divine One, you are a powerful creator of worlds and new realities whether you know it or not. Through your words, your thoughts, energy and aligned action you transform the Universe and that ability to create is amplified when you are in alignment with truth. When your thoughts, words and energy are all in resonance your Divine Will is active and it is through the actions aligned with that Divine Will that you create miracles. In each moment and each day you have the ability to transform your reality, to choose to not be defined by your current circumstance but rather to step into your Divinity and consciously choose what you want to experience. As you turn within and get clear on the desires of your heart, and you release the ways of the past that no longer align with you and take conscious and intentional action everything will change. Allow yourself to step into the frequency of belief and the receiving of miracles and watch in wonder and awe of all that takes place.

135.

Divine One, be here now, present with all that is and ever was, present to your innate knowing, your magic, you worth, and your divinity. You are a cosmic, conscious being, energy in human form and you can access your expansive consciousness in any moment by simply coming back to the Now. As you become aware of your expansive nature and breathe in the infinite Universe, knowing YOU ARE ONE, you will fully embody that powerful life force energy and begin to utilize it to create worlds. Through your Divine Will, Open Heart, and Inspired Action anything is possible as you tune into the love and grace present in each and every moment. As you slow down to notice the vibrations of energy all around you and embrace the experiences of this life you will begin to notice deep peace, pleasure, and connection taking up acreage in your heart, spreading like a wildfire throughout all you encounter and this life will begin to feel like the magical masterpiece it is. You simply get to choose it.

136.

Divine One, you are the breath, you are the trees, you are the bird and you are the bees. You are within and of each and every microcosm of the universe. You are it all and it All is you. Today I ask you to zoom out on life, to see the kaleidoscope vision of this life and every other, to transcend time and space and see just how small your current physical existence truly is. And now zoom all the way in, to the tiniest cell in your body and sense the entirety of the Universe alive within it. And fill within how it's all connected, all woven together in this beautiful fabric of existence. And as you become One with all that is, allow yourSelf to Live in alignment with this knowing, to slow down in the day to day and take time for the little things. And know in each moment, you are loved, cherished and held.

137.

Divine One, this life is a beautiful gift. In each and every moment you are experiencing a cosmic dance between human and divine. In each moment you have the ability to harness the power of the present and ride the waves of life into a beautiful future. In each moment life is; showing you, teaching you, transforming you. It is up to you whether you listen and move with ease or you resist and attempt control. When you step back from the programs and limitations of the world and realize that all you truly desire is Here, Now and that happiness, joy, and peace are frequencies always available at your core, you can sink into the freedom of the moment and all your worries simply fall away. When you can drop the need to try, to have, to hustle and control- miracles happen for and through you. Life responds to your frequency, to the peace in your heart and Love of your Soul. In this moment Be Here Now, find gratitude for everything present and know you are loved. In this place you will see the magnificent gift that is Life.

138.

Divine One, each and every experience, every circumstance, every sensation is simply an opportunity to feel, evolve, explore, something new. When you can view life from the lens of the now and embrace each and every moment with awe and wonder then even your deepest grief can be "enjoyed" You can walk into uncomfortable moments and experience them fully with the understanding that you are Universal Consciousness having the experience of that sensation. Rather than taking it personally or attaching deep meaning to each event and emotion that arises simply feel, honor, fully Live it and in its own time it will pass and you repeat again with what comes next. It's when we take life too seriously and try to attach meaning to every experience big or small that the mind begins to create stories. That we begin to cling to or resist the present moment and therefore tarnish it;s exquisite nature and create undo suffering for ourselves. As you approach this new day breathe, feel, be and notice what life is teaching you in each lived experience and know that it too, is Love.

139.

Divine One, you are all that is and ever was and all that is to come. You are the stars, the moon, the mountains, the rain. You are everything. It's in that knowing, that love, compassion, connection, and creation come with ease. A knowing that when you serve the world you serve yourSelf and when you serve yourSelf you serve the world. Each and every moment, actions, experience is a collective one, an opportunity to expand into Universal Oneness and come into alignment as a Divine humanity. It's a knowing that each moment is happening for you and for the greater good. That both the hard moments and the joy filled ones are once in a lifetime opportunities to go within and experience life with a new perspective, an expanded knowing, and a deep sense of being. It's with your breath, your presence that you align with this way. So breathe, be, and remember that We Are One.

140.

Divine One, in this moment right here and right now you are loved, you are safe, you are held. Deepen into your breath and allow the peace to encompass you. Feel the light and warmth all around you and know that this is available to you at all times. You are a powerful being having a beautiful experience, it is only your mind that makes those experiences wrong or bad, it is only you mind that creates perceived separation and suffering, only your mind that creates stories of perceived outcomes that bring you away from the truth of this moment. But as your Breathe Divine One, you align with the Universal Consciousness and if only for a moment those stories fall away. As you practice mindfulness and conscious breathing you can live more and more of this life without the stories getting in the way, you can simply experience each moment for the beauty that it is. In doing this you experience existential peace and deepen your alignment with truth. So breathe, Be and know that here and now you are Love.

141.

Divine One, there is much darkness in the world… But there is MORE light. Love is a powerful force that will lead humanity out of even the most trying and destructive times. As you focus on the Love in your own heart and work to embody that love and raise your own vibration you have a massive effect on the collective consciousness. Now is a time of a huge energetic purge. The darkness of the world, the lower vibrational energies, and those that are unconscious are being jolted awake; given the choice to join us in Love or create further division. Now more than ever the power of love in each sovereign individual is being awakened and radiated outward. Many are experiencing physical effects as their body changes on a physical level in order to hold this new frequency. Many are facing the parts of themSelves that no longer serve them. We ask you to hold the light, to remain grounded and steady and know this too shall pass. Remain steadfast and be the beacon for those awakening now. The Golden Age is coming. We must encircle the remaining darkness into the light.

142.

Divine One, you are the light of this world. You have the ability to transmute even the darkest energies into love. You have the ability to expand your own energetic field wider and brighter to maintain high frequencies of energy for this world. You are a powerful change agent, here to usher in the new world and with each moment, each breathe, each act of heart centered service to yourself and the world you are creating great change. As you sink into the energy of oneness with it all that is and ever was and allow yourself to tune into the highest frequencies of love you swallow up the darkness, making space for it, too, within your field. In your acceptance and love for this darkness and chaos you transform it into life-force energy and through aligned action and Divine Will can create even more Goodness and Beauty on this Earth. Life is a series of choices and when you align your choices with Love you expand that love to encompass the whole world. As we all come together to create this great change we create a lasting effect on humanity and the lives of all present in the Earth here and now. This is how we create with light.

143.

Divine One, you are here on this planet at this particular time for a reason. Your gifts, talents, and sacred energies are needed here to raise the collective consciousness of the planet and create the New Earth. You have shown great courage as you have rooted into faith and lead the way for so many others. We have watched you rise and rise again through some of the hardest times in your life and continue to choose love. Thank you for that, thank you for all you have done for the world, you are truly a gift to this planet. As we usher in the new energies of possibility and hope and stand in a powerful portal of reality creation we ask you to keep your head held high, to dream big, and go all in. The current energies on earth will allow manifestations to occur almost instantaneously, what you plant now will be plentiful come next spring. Remember the gift of the seasons; they are here as a reminder to pace yourself, to honor each cycle of this human experience. The end of autumn and beginning of the winter months is a time for collective hibernation, to rest and steadily build reserves of energy as you enter the dream state more often and consciously cultivate your energy field for the coming year. Use this time to be with the hope and possibility alive on Earth now and dream a little bigger. Everything is about to change.

144.

Divine One, as you follow your joy and the inspiration of your heart you find life gets easy. Miracles, synchronicities and Universal Support becomes apparent around every corner. Not because they aren't always there but because when you follow your joy you are more tuned into the Universal frequencies and can therefore see the manifestation of that vibration all around you. Society has pulled you away from your truth, from your Higher Self and that is why it feels so scary to simply follow your joy. Your mind and ego will attempt to remind you of all the perceived failures, rejections, and doubts that could follow if you don't stay in line with the status quo and that's only because that is what your ego has seen as safe up until this point. But Divine One, the way humanity operates now is NOT the way it was meant to and it's not the way it will continue to operate. It takes individual souls like you making the courageous decision to forge their own path that will create a new way for humanity, a way where each person follows the joy of their own hearts, a way of coming together, fair exchange, community, peace and Love. With one brave soul at a time this Earth will be transformed. So we say to you today, are you Willing to follow your joy?

145.

Divine One, in a world plagued by the hustle you will hear the desperate pleas of your Soul to slow down. For, your Soul, your Essence, your Light, knows that it is the Being that shapes the doing. It is in the rest we create the most and in the slowing down that allows for clarity and ease to come forward. In your society many things are backwards and most of that is on purpose. It's in the efforts of the one's deemed "in charge" to pull you away from your power, your essence, your creative insights and super powers. When you are constantly consumed with the day to day, with the getting ahead and getting more, there is little room to do anything other than survive. The ultimate life hack is to slow down, to create space to get clear and disconnect from all around you. When you make space to simply be with what is the next step will automatically make itself known to you, there will be no hustle, no striving, no controlling, just a sense of ease as you move from the heart centered knowing within, the wisdom of your Soul. So today, at this moment can you make time to simply Be, to feel the Ease? It is there you will find every answer you seek.

146.

Divine One, life on Earth is one colossal collaboration. It is your relationship with each and everything around you that defines you and the life you are living. The rocks on the river only exist because you perceive them to, the sounds you hear only exist because of the vibrations they create in your ear drum, the words you speak only exist to those who receive them. Without relationship nothing exists. And you are here on Earth to relate to each person, place and experience through your unique lens. In doing so you evolve the Soul. At any point your perception of self or other can change and be born again brand new. The answer to every perceived struggle, obstacle or fear is to come back to what part of you is creating the current perception of it. And as you evolve eventually you will embody the knowing that you are One with everything around you and so you see that every aspect of every relationship is at the core a relationship with your true Self. Each way you respond or react to something outside of yourself shows you a deeper truth hidden within You. Relationships are how we evolve and grow in this human experience. As you see the world through the lens of eternal connection you will see the world as Love.

147.

Divine One, each and every being on Earth has their own unique blueprint, their own soul song if you will. The way their unique code responds to the frequencies of life composes their symphony and as you master the chords of your soul you can tune into higher frequencies, create expanded life songs, and move through the ebb and flow of this life with more ease. And while everyone has their own unique patterns that create magnificent and unique versions of life each and everyone is connected to the same Source. The energy that brings life (consciousness) to every single person, place and things is One in the Same. And it's in consciously returning to that Oneness while honoring your own individual patterns and rhythms that allow you to expand into all that you are. As you realize that you are a unique extension of Source energy a new sense of power and freedom is born. A knowing of your limitless nature allows you to expand into your highest potential, a knowing of the One true Source allows you to feel safe and held in each moment of each day, and the knowing that we are all connected to the same sweet flow of energy will allow you to live from love, viewing each interaction as an opportunity to know and love thyself through another again and again. Live boldly sweet one, compose your masterpiece, contribute to the Universal Symphony and let yourself dance freely through life as you do it. It's simply not that serious. It gets to be fun.

148.

Divine One, you are perfect and worthy just as you are. I know at times the weight of the world and the expectations formed from your limited perspective can sometimes cause you to feel separate and lost. Especially now as we end this cycle and step into a new paradigm of love and connection all the parts of you in this and all lifetimes are coming forward to be seen, loved, and integrated. It can feel heavy and hard to move into a space of love and compassion as you face all the parts of yourself you have deemed unworthy but we want you to know that this is all part of the process and it will soon pass. As you can take time to slow down and shine the light on the darkest parts of you in time you will experience the most wholesome and enlivening energy of love you've ever felt. It is this energy that we are collectively anchoring in as we move into the New Earth. We have done the work to clear the weeds and create space and now we will consciously choose and a collective the kind of world we wish to create. So breathe into yourself and find love for all that you are. Soon it will be time to walk in a new way.

149.

Divine One, remember, you are pure consciousness in a human vessel. Your energy, intention, and thoughts amplify the energy around you and materialize in your waking reality. As you master your inner world your outer world matches it. That is how you create your own personal reality. When your beliefs, thoughts and energy come into alignment and you move forward with Divine Will literally anything you can conceive is possible. That is how you master yourSelf and this world, by bringing into awareness your thoughts and beliefs and matching those with your actions and energy. You are so much more than you can currently comprehend and the possibilities are utterly limitless as you stand fully in your truth and knowing. You have the ability to alchemize and transform any situation, feeling and circumstance into anything you desire. It takes discipline, awareness and a true understanding of the depths of our existence. You will begin to see fully as you live from your higher consciousness and Divine Mind rather than the Ego. Life is a series of choices you make. Making choices in alignment with your highest truth creates waking dreams and magic realities.

150.

Divine One, the stillness found in the present moment is one of the most powerful portals available to you in the human experience. It allows you to sink into the magic and beauty of what is here, now, available to you in each moment. As you find yourself present with what is, you are able to cultivate profound gratitude for each experience, raising your vibration and attracting more of what you desire. When you drop into a state of intentional presence all allow life to be a ritual you are able to evolve, grow, and create from each lived experience whether or not you have labeled it good or bad. You are able to harness the energy of the now to create a reality in alignment with your heart's desires. Present moment intention allows you to lead with love for yourself and others, it breaks barriers, shatters the limitations of the mind and expands you into a frequency of limited possibility. Today breathe life into the present moment, find reverence for the here and now and watch as your reality shifts in the direction of your dreams.

151.

Divine One, you are a Divine Being with unlimited power and energy. As you tap into the wellspring of energy within you you also activate a deep and sacred knowing. As your Masculine and Feminine energy learn to dance in harmony with one another your energy field comes into perfect alignment. The sacred and life giving energy within each being is what sustains your energy in this waking reality. Deep inner knowing, trust, and wisdom come from this place. As you learn to trust your intuition and take aligned action based on Divine Will rather than the ego your life will radically change. You will break free from the matrix and begin to experience life as it was meant to be. A primal and intuitive nature will rise and a deep sense of trust for Self and Source will be born. You have the ability to access this knowing and way of being in any moment but it is something you must consciously choose and learn to cultivate. Sink into your inner wisdom today, begin to listen to your body's intuitive knowing and move from awe and wonder as you break away from all that binds your infinite knowledge.

152.

Divine One, can you let the grounding energies of the Earth support you in this transitional time? In moments of fear can you feel your feet on the ground and ask, "Earth mother, root me into safety?" In moments of perceived lack can you feel your feet on the ground and say "Earth mother, root me into my abundance?" In moments of anxiety can you feel your feet on the ground and say "Earth Mother, root me into peace?" As we calibrate to the new earth you must also root into the frequencies you desire to carry forward with you. Breathe deep into your knowing, stay connected to your divinity and consciously choose what you are rooting into. The Earth wants to provide for you, to protect you, to nurture and unburden you, but you must let her.

153.

Divine One, allow yourSelf to feel all that stirs within, make space, open to every sensation, every experience but don't let it consume you… rather… Remember what you are. Allow yourSelf to step back into the place of the observer, the one listening to the thoughts, the one noticing the sensations, the one watching the behavior, and instead of attaching yourSelf what is taking place, learn from it, step back from it and allow yourSelf to expand, allowing it to unfold before you but not consume you. It's from your conscious observation that you can alchemize and create a new, it's from there you can intentionally anchor into joy, happiness, abundance and wonder despite what is occurring in your external world. It's from there you unlock the key to eternal happiness and reality creation. So breathe, step back, and enjoy the show. PS- You're the lead role.

154.

Divine One, can you let us surprise you? Can you let go of all the ways you think it should be, think it could be and simply allow it to be as is? We have wondrous, magnificent miracles in store for you however they are not going to show up the way you think they are. How could they? These miracles are meant for your highest, your best, a version of you that you haven't even met yet, so how could you possibly fathom how and what we have in store for you? Those dreams and desires you have… Divine One, we will amplify them times ten, you will be awestruck, simply blown away by the magnitude of blessing coming your way, but we need you to release control, to release all preconceived ideas and notions and simply allow them to happen for and through you. That is the only way. So breathe, let go of the ways of the old and prepare to be inspired by the new. It is time.

155.

Divine One, love is what you are, it is the frequency at which pure consciousness resides. It was only upon entering your human form that your current perception, projection and even reaction to that love around you changed. And it was supposed to; you are here having a human experience so you can evolve more fully into love. So that you can learn to bring even the darkest and most doubt filled parts of yourself into that love. So that you can, despite any human conditioning, remember that you are never separate from that which you are, that you are never alone and that you are pure and worthy in each moment. It's in honoring, accepting and purely loving yourself and all around you that you will step into the full remembrance of your conscious form and Divine One, it is that collective remembering that will change the course of humanity forever and therefore change the world. So if you "do" anything today… Be the Love.

156.

Divine One, big deep breaths and know you are Love. It is time to start gathering, time to start building, time to BE THE CHANGE. We have the numbers what we lack is organization. You are being called to RISE IN LOVE and LEAD the way to the New Earth. To gather your people, to ignite the Revolution of Love and to begin building the new Earth we all so desperately need. We know it might feel scary, that taking the lead and walking in faith isn't easy but DIvine One, you know you were meant for this, built for this meticulously positioned and prepared for this and now is the time. Unless we come together united in love things will remain the same. The old has already began to crumble, it is a ripe playing field for new seeds to be planted. And it is up to us as a collective to initiate change. So we ask you, be brave, walk in love, and ignite change.

157.

Divine One, love is always the answer.
Pure and unconditional love for yourSelf and for the world.
Love means the end of all suffering, the end of all wars, the end of all pain.
Love is the answer.
As you move forward today and all days can you ask yourSelf,
"What would love do? What would love say? How would love be?"
And as the answers come, can you emulate LOVE?
Because Divine One, as you sink deeper into the love that you are… the entire world will change.

158.

Divine One, your purpose in life is not some end result or label.
It's not some deep passion or sense of direction.
Your only true purpose in life is living; being present in the here and now.
Being present and open to each and every experience you encounter.
So many people spend countless hours of their life searching for all the things outside themselves, striving for some made up version of success or achievement only to find themselves circling the drain feeling empty and confused.
Society has created that illusion on purpose, to keep you from your power, to keep you from your essence.
The essence and power that can only be found in the profound acceptance of the here and now.
Divine One, you are living your purpose right now with each breath you take with each experience you have with every sensation you feel.
So take a deep breath, let go of the expectations and ideals and let yourself experience the magic and this moment here now.

159.

What if we allowed our walls to simply come down
If we stopped trying so hard to protect ourSelves and instead simply knew… we were divinely protected.
What if we let go of our perceived control
If we let it go and simply allowed ourSelves to walk through life in deep submission (internal power) to all that was and all that will be.
What if we dropped our judgements
If we simply lived knowing we were one, the same consciousness in different vessels and we treated ourSelves, our friends, our neighbors and even strangers with sacred love and reverence.
What if we dropped the conditions we've place on happiness and love
If we claimed our divine right to constant inner happiness, peace and love despite what happened outside of us and used our energy to harness and cultivate more and more inner peace and happiness for ourSelves each and every moment of each and every day.
What if we decided to live from the knowing that Universal Consciousness IS what we are…
and allowed the human experience to be just that… An EXPERIENCE in this life, to learn to grow and stopped attaching so much weight to all the things outside of our Eternal "Mind"
What if we simply allowed ourselves to be all that we are… All we have always been..

160.

I asked God why
Why all the pain. The abuse, the suffering?
Why the big heart and feeling body?
Why can't I just shut it off and become cold?
Why do I keep attracting those who wish to cause me harm?
And why do I continue to hold them in love?
Why does my heart feel stretched by humanities hurts?
Why do I feel such a deep call to incite change?
Why can't I just let it all go? Turn a blind eye? Why do I have to care soooo f^cking much?!
Why...
And she said, "because Divine One, you chose to lead.
You chose to walk the path so others wouldn't have to… at least not in the same way.
You chose to feel, to heal, to love and to evolve
You chose to become increasingly tender with every blow
You chose to have your heart stretched by both grief and love
You chose to master alchemy and with that came attempt after attempt of turning the pain into pleasure
You chose to forge a path of light so others might not have to hurt the way you did.
You chose to remember what you really are so you could see through the illusion and into the magic
You chose to lead the great revolution into the New Earth.
You chose.
And you're doing it Divine One, keep moving forward. I've got you.
It's almost over.
All of this is part of the greater plan. You might not see it now… but it's all unfolding exactly as it needs to.
Breathe. Keep your faith. And continue to do the work. "

161.

Divine One, I am wrapping you in love and grace and envisioning you in the knowing that who and how you are right now is absolutely perfect.
Regardless of the sensations you are experiencing or circumstances you perceive please know this…
YOU ARE NEVER ALONE.
You are being held, guided, and provided for each and every step of the way.
As you learn to let go and deepen into the here and now the external chatter will fall away and you will once again remember the truth within you.
You Divine One are a powerful soul having a human experience and what you experience here on Earth does not define you.
Breathe and let yourself feel it all fully and soon it will pass.

162.

"Don't ask what the world needs…Ask what makes you come alive"

This life is our opportunity to discover every piece of ourselves, to strengthen ourselves, and to prepare ourselves to return "home" as the divine beings we are.

As we go through life many of us forget one critical aspect of our journey here on earth and that is, to find inner and lasting joy. Joy that comes from within us.

Oftentimes we live our lives asking what the world needs, meanwhile denying ourselves the inner joy we so desperately long for. This causes inner resentment and anger.

Once we are filled with those heavy emotions we are unable to connect to our higher selves and show up the way we are meant to in the world.

By seeking what makes us come alive we better serve ourselves and in turn the world. By finding our own bliss we make the world a better place.

What makes you come alive?

163.

Divine One, as you release what no longer serves you, all that never really did, you make space within for more of all that you desire.
You make space for the new versions of you to grow, space for healthy love, space for expanded wealth. We know it can feel scary and hard to say goodbye to an old way of being, to a relationship that represented a piece of who you were, even to a job or experience, but we also know as you cling to the old and outdated versions of Self you suppress your Soul, your essence, your magic. You suppress the very parts of you that are begging to come to life. And after years of doing this all that old energy gets trapped in your body and it's hard to even remember the magic and divinity that dwells within. Divine One, we know this is scary, but we promise it's worth it.

164.

Divine One, it's time, here and now to let go. To Make a choice. Will you break the cycle, or do it over again? If you're seeing this I know you are choosing to break free, choosing yourSelf above all else, choosing to live and love in alignment with your best and highest and I know it's painful, I know it feels like part of you is dying and you just don't want to let go. But sweet one I also know what's on the other side, the bliss and freedom that comes from the soul aching liberation. Be gentle but fierce as you walk the path into the unknown and know this.. Each and every step of the way you are loved, cherished, and supported. And you are doing a really good job.

165.

Divine One, breathe and know all is well. There may be many shadows and patterns coming up right now, so many distractions and ways to avoid the truth of the present moment. But Divine One, these are all stories your ego and past self are telling you. You can choose to clear your mind and move from the present in any moment, you can choose to align more deeply with your heart and soul and turn to God/Source.Universe for all things. You do not have to carry this weight on your own, you do not have to silence your voice. You can speak your needs loud and clear and open wide to receive them and you will be met with the most Divine grace and nurturance you've ever experienced. We encourage you to deepen into yourSelf today, to have a good belly laugh, spend some time in nature and drink plenty of water. Life is shifting drastically and it's up to you to respond in alignment with what feels true to your heart.

166.

Divine One, life is an adventure. Let it be. Let yourSelf run wild with passion, follow excitement and expand into the edges of your Soul and beyond. This life is meant to be lived fully, to be experienced from head to toe, soul to bone, pleasure and pain, darkness and light. Risks are meant to be taken, rules and meant to be shattered, and hearts meant to lead the way. Let yourSelf live fully knowing the pureness of your soul and the expansive nature of your heart's love. Divine One, we want nothing more than you to take full advantage of the human experience in this form. Move away from the labels and expectations the world has cast onto you and breathe life into something new. What have you got to lose?

167.

Divine One, more than anything we hope you know that here and now you are loved, deeply and divinely and unconditionally.

This human experience isn't for the faint of heart. You chose to incarnate at this time knowing it would push you to your depths, knowing you'd be edged out in every direction and you chose it anyway.

You chose it knowing you'd be coming to a strange land in an even stranger body.

You chose it knowing you would at sometimes forget what you truly are, you chose it knowing that a veil of separation would be lifted between you and your soul's knowing.

You chose it knowing you would face darkness and grief and pain.

You chose it knowing your ego would die and be reborn again and again in one lifetime.

You chose it knowing it would hurt.

But Divine One you also chose it knowing you were serving humanity, that you were evolving Source consciousness itSelf, knowing you were expanding into deeper depths of love and grace than you had ever previously known.

You chose it knowing you can never truly be separate from that which you came.

You chose it knowing you would one day return and remember the all prevailing love.

You chose it knowing it would be worth it.

So Divine One, breathe and know no matter what you are experiencing right now you knew you'd make it through and you saw the bigger picture of the change that would take place Universally because of your choice to Be Here Now.

168.

Divine One, where you are here and now is perfect. There is no where else you need to be. As you learn to surrender to this moment you will find magic and beauty in each piece of life. As you learn to lean into the present, you will see a world of endless possibility and your heart will lead the way. So breathe into yourSelf, breathe into your feet on the ground and set the intention to be Here, Now, throughout this day, wherever and however it may be, let it be enough. And watch as the mysteries of the universe unfold before you.

169.

Divine One, things continue to shift on Earth at a rapid rate. You can see a clear change in humanity; those who are asleep and those who have opened their eyes to the truth of this world. Massive solar flares and energies will continue to flood through the Earth's atmosphere preparing your body to hold even more light, you are being prepared for what is to come. If you are experiencing the highs, continue to let it flow, continue to expand and breathe into this luscious new energy as your heart space stretches even wider. If you are still struggling to integrate and experiencing ascension symptoms like heightened emotions, body aches, exhaustion, headaches and more, continue to ground and release; hydrate and let the stored emotions leave your body so the light can integrate. Wherever you are at, on your journey know that you are right on "time" and continue to trust in the unfolding of the timeline shift and new earth creation.

170.

Divine One, open your heart to feel all that is present. Even if it feels like your heart might break under the pressure of these heightened senses, let yourself open wide. Your emotions are like a cleansing fire, purifying and transmuting all the emotional and energetic debris you have been storing in your body. When you simply let your emotions flow through you without attaching a story, without attaching labels or judgment, simply letting them be felt, heard, witnessed, they will cleanse and dissolve, leaving you in an expanded clear knowing state. Be brave enough to feel what is arising and know that it too, is love.

171.

Divine One, as you breathe into each moment, calling your power, energy, and Divine Will into the here and now you will experience the fullness of your being. No longer split and divided into pockets of leaked energy you will experience the entirety of your ability, the entirety of your energetic bank. And as you become conscious and aware of what you give your power and energy too you become more intentional with those investments. Every interaction, every trigger/activation, every story, every emotion is an energetic investment into something outside of yourSelf. Everything you say Yes to means saying no to something else. We ask you for today, to be mindful of where you are investing your energy, be mindful as you call it back to you, and move from the fullness of your being. When you operate from a full energetic bank and intentionally invest in what you truly desire, those dreams materialize into the physical world at a much faster rate and you feel good throughout the whole process.

172.

Divine One, you are more needed on the earth at this time than you might realize. We are amidst a powerful shift in timelines, a shift that will divide those who chose to stay with the ways of the old and those who choose the New Earth. And Divine One, as you step into the New Earth frequencies we are calling on you to build, create, and live in harmony with these new frequencies. Each and every being who chooses this way makes a huge difference in the collective transformation. Every single being matters when it comes to the expansion and materialization of the New Earth timeline and we are counting on you to maintain the vibration of love and integrity with Self/Source in all you do. This is a time to stay connected to Higher Consciousness to constantly remember what you are and live according to your hearts knowing. When you turn within and listen to the silence you will know the way, you will be guided to the next best step. This is a time for trust, surrender, and aligned action. We love you.

173.

Divine One, as you breathe deep into this moment, let yourself land fully in this body and then while grounded in it, let yourSelf expand. Let yourSelf expand into the infinite space of the Universe and know that it is all you. This human experience is one small fragment in perceived time and space. But in actuality each one of us is One. It is only our physical experience that creates that perceived separation and the forgetting of the Divine within. The more you allow yourself to expand into it all the greater your light body becomes and the greater your capacity to hold that alchemizing, life transforming energy. It is in your focus on the energy over matter, your focus on how you desire to feel, your focus on faith and love and miracles that will cause a great chasm to occur within thus shifting your entire waking reality. The act of going inward, of visualizing, feeling and knowing positive things about the future will make a great and more lasting impact on your current situation than any amount doing ever could. So today, play, day dream, know in your heart that things are shifting for your benefit, and watch how your reality changes.

174.

Divine One, love is the answer. Your love, your energy, your light. These are the things to invest in. These are the things to hold sacred, knowing as you focus inward you amplify these powerful energies and one act in faith at a time you change the world. This is a time to go within, to focus on the desires of your heart and expand your field of consciousness into the vast Universal energies. Divine One, remember this, you are an extension of Source energy, you are a Divine Being in a human vessel and you have all the knowledge and knowing within you. As you steady your mind and harmonize with your heart you will see clearly the way, you will see the beauty in the here and now and you will know the love that resides in every fiber of your being. You Divine One are a sacred gem, you Divine One, are the key to it all.

175.

A reminder that you are worthy right here, right now. There is nothing you have to do, no one you have to be, nothing that needs achieved. You are simply worthy in each moment, in each sensation, in each vibration and experience regardless of how you perceive it.
Your connection to Source consciousness never fades, you can never be separate from that which you are.
And Divine One…
You ARE pure Source Consciousness.
You ARE love
You ARE wealth
You ARE health
You ARE connection
You ARE here
You ARE there
You ARE nothing &
You ARE everything
You ARE life
You ARE the cosmos
You ARE the earth
It's in remembering all that you are and LIVING, BEING, BREATHING from that knowing that you will see your outer reality match your inner dreams. All you seek is one shift in embodied being away.
Live it
Breathe it
Know it
You are WORTHY, ALIGNED, and LOVED
Here, Now, and Always.

176.

Divine One, can you open up to the idea that you are being taken care of, that you are being protected, positioned, and provided for in each moment. Can you open to receive the gifts, bounties, and blessings the Universe desires to pour into you? Can you simply be with it all regardless of how it aligns with what you expected and know that what is here now is perfect? Can you enjoy the simple moments in life how they are? Can you kick your head back in laughter and smile until your jaw aches? It's these sweet and small moments of unadulterated joy, bliss, and present moment gratitude that shift you into a higher frequency, a frequency where abundance and love are the norm and inner peace is the foundation. And Divine One, it's up to you to choose it, here now, with whatever might be present in front of you. We know it might not be exactly what you wanted but we also want you to remember that as you sink into joy and gratitude for what you currently have and experience, your desires will continue to be amplified and expanded. So today, laugh, smile, be, follow the joy.

177.

Divine One, there is an entire world of possibilities at your fingertips, a world of people waiting to meet YOU, a host of support, miracles, and blessings that are yours to receive as you understand what you truly are and how to utilize your abilities to the fullest.
We can't live from our highest self when we still wear the armor of the world.
When our inner child is draped in trauma, limiting beliefs, and fears our highest self is sometimes out of reach.
When our shadows are masked and hidden our higherSelf is filtered and dimmed.
Until we stand in full acceptance of it all , until our inner children learn of the innate magic they possess, we remain stuck in a chapter written by the world, while our adventure remains unwritten.
This work promises freedom, confidence, empowerment. It means deep inner peace, clarity of mind and a vision of your future that becomes more and more real everyday.
This work means living life fully alive, honoring your divinity while in human form. Standing in human form, fully aware of your Divinity.
It means...having it all.

178.

Divine One, when you pray or simply speak to the Universe do so knowing that your words are being heard. And when we say knowing…Really know it. Walk away from your prayer and live as if whatever you found gratitude for will be amplified, knowing whatever you requested will be brought into your life, know mentally, emotionally, physically and spiritually that your desires will become reality. This is how you walk in faith, this is how you create your dreams. Ask and know it is being provided. It is in that knowing that you will be inspired to take aligned action to receive that desired outcome. Use prayer with this level of intention and focus and you will change your entire life.

179.

Divine One, expand into love, expand into knowing, expand into peace. In times of doubt, fear and even joy sink into the deepest depths and highest heights of your expansion. You do this by first grounding in, aligning with your breath, and focusing your mind's eye on higher consciousness, become the consciousness you are, expand as big and as infinitely as the Universe and simply breathe. As you sink deeper into this connection feel the electric energy move through your system, feel the bliss, the joy, the calm and know that in that moment you are fully yourSelf, fully in alignment with truth. And when you return to your physical reality carry this knowing and expansion with you. Throughout the day you will feel the way you are held and cared for in each moment.

180.

Divine One, many of you are purging on a massive scale right now and even experiencing physical symptoms as a result of these changes. Letting go of each and every past way of being, your heart may be breaking as these past lives are showing up in your mind's eye and we want you to know it's almost over. This is part of the integration and evolution process. Hold steady, talk openly about your experience, you will find many are in the same place, and take care of your human vessel with grounding, proper nutrition and hydration. As your physical body expands its capacity to hold the light you will continue to feel it. Stay conscious, stay steady and know you are loved.

181.

Divine One, your physical body is currently undergoing great changes. Skin, brains, and even bones are evolving to adapt to your new light body. The capacity to hold Divine Light in a physical plane is not an easy one, and for those of you who have been on the path for quite some time are noticing many symptoms of this change. Foggy and pressurized heads, neck and shoulder pain, sinus fatigue, abdominal and digestive symptoms, for gendered females womb healing has taken place. And many more. These symptoms will pass soon as your physical body adapts to the new way of light and the increased light energy within your field. The best thing you can do right now is ground and hydrate and connect to this higher consciousness as often as possible through meditation and aligned energy. Breathe deep into yourself and listen to your body. You are doing a really good job.

182.

Divine One, we know this time on earth isn't always easy, we know it's hard to keep the faith and focus on the light before you when there is so much darkness but we also know how powerful you are, how powerful the suggested thoughts of your mind become as you invest energy into their reality. Divine One, at any moment you can shift how you feel and what you see, in any moment you can alchemize the things you don't desire into more of what you do, in any moment you can choose to feel good., held and loved, even amidst life's chaos. We want you to know that you are innately worthy, good, and cared for in all moments. When you consciously choose to connect to the Divine support around you, you will see it. Like the old adage goes, first you must believe it.

183.

Divine One, breathe deep into yourself for a moment and take an energetic step back. As feelings of self judgment and perceived inferiority arise, know this… if no one else existed you would have no one to compare yourself to. You'd therefore believe that who and how you are is perfect or at the very least acceptable. You place your worth and value on how you felt inside rather than looking towards others for that value and worth. So in essence when you judge yourself you're only judging yourself based on comparison with another therefore giving your power away, placing your worth in your perception of them and their perception of you. When you reclaim that power and focus on how you feel about you based on your inner essence you will find you are infinitely worthy and whole in this moment now.

184.

Divine One, you are a powerful Earth Warrior, A Cosmic and Infinite being of love and light and you are here for a reason. You chose this lifetime, this experience, these earthly circumstances. You chose to lead, to alchemize, to be a beacon of hope for others, the way shower of the world. You chose it all, and we know it hasn't been easy, we know your heart has been broken by this world more times than you can count and we now sometimes the doubt has become more than you could take, and yet you are still here, still choosing yourSelf, still choosing love, still choosing grace and that Divine One is why WE chose YOU. We promise, it's almost over. And your time to shine, to become all you've ever desired to be is right around the corner, see it, feel it, be it now and know that we are with you always.

185.

Divine One, I know it's so easy to lean into the idea that there is something bigger and more magnificent out there waiting to catch you…
But it's not what you think.
God/Source/Universe…
Baby, that's YOU.
It's YOU who causes the Sun to rise and the Moon to Shine
You who creates the waves that ripple across the vast landscapes"
You: the trees, the birds, the snow and the rain.
It's YOU.
The one you depend on
The one to whom you pray
The one you try so gallantly to be "good" for
It's YOU.
You are both the alter and the prayer.
The one who submits
And the one you submit too.
It's YOU.

186.

Divine One, I want you to feel this. Know this. Live this.
You are highly favored. The Universe wants, more than anything else, for you to reside in a state of grace, bliss, and joy.
The human experience can feel rough sometimes, I know. Things happen that create pain, doubt, and fear.
Words and experiences poke our triggers and our hurt inner children, our rejected shadows, our egos, sometimes take over and create more pain.
But those feelings don't cancel out the infinite and eternal love that resides within, no, that Divine One, is what you are made of, it's what you are at your core.
All emotions are simply surges of energy telling us whether or not something or someone is in alignment with the highest good of our soul, but instead of taking them for what they are (information pointing us back to ourSelves)
We sometimes attach to these emotions and start to believe that they are in charge.
When you can learn to witness the way energy moves through you, the way that your emotions speak to you and learn how to alchemize it into more of what you want you become the highest versions of yourself here on earth, no longer run by wounds or shadows, simply walking through the human experience as the Divine Being you are.
It doesn't mean hard things won't happen, but what it does mean is when they do you will approach it from your divinity, you'll see it as an opportunity to harness more energy and therefore create more of what you want.
You'll feel more joy, more love, more ease. You'll choose those things in alignment with your soul without a doubt and second thought. You'll walk this earth, truly free.

187.

Divine One,
Let your heart break wide open
Feel it all
As the stories of the past, the worries of the future fall away.
Honoring what is.
Make room for the new as you stand in awe and gratitude of the present moment.
Breathe, baby, breathe.
Something beautiful and miraculous is moving through you.
But you can't take the old reality into the new one.
It's time to rise in the glory of love, Divine Union, and joy.
Your heart will lead the way
If you let it.

188.

Divine One, you are the way, life is the teacher.
As you move through life you are given opportunities to look at yourself, at your life, at your choices.
When you find peace with your way of being you are set free.
When you can release the shame and guilt from your heart it becomes light as a feather and you ascend into heaven, into the frequency of Christ Consciousness from which we all came.
As you move into forgiveness for self and others and truly embody unconditional acceptance for all you will be freed from the shackles of society and walk in the New Earth.
We came here to pave the way for a new way of being, for the embodiment of love and the deepest universal truths.
So ask yourself, what weighs heavily on my heart and how can I release it?

189.

Divine One, take a deep breath in and sink into the here and now. Today is a new day, a new month, a new opportunity to consciously choose who and how you want to be and what you want to create.
It's an opportunity to wipe the slate clean and start anew.
This is a powerful time of love and creation on the Earth.
The energies are higher than ever as more and more souls awaken and shift the balance of humanity.
This is a time to listen to your body; to trust the need for rest and the need for movement throughout each day. This is the time to release the standards of society and the ways of the old and harness the collective energy. The New Earth timeline is one of Being, where joy and wonder are found in the slowing down and the most magnificent creations are birther from rest. It's a time for connection, community and a simpler kind of life. As we all come together and choose the soft and slow life it will become the new normal and the collective nervous system can relax and regulate once and for all, it's from there true power and embodiment is found. So breathe, be at ease, and give yourself permission to enjoy the natural pace of each moment.

190.

Divine One, each moment in your life is happening in perfect timing.
As you sink into trust for the unfolding of all you desire you will see the perfection and grace in each lived experience.
If things are happening slower then you desire trust that you are being prepared and positioned for the perfect outcome.
If things are happening faster then you feel ready for trust that you are being propelled into a new timeline.
Whatever is occurring in your life, at whatever pace, know it is right on time.
When you step out of the way and release control and expectations you make room for miracles beyond your wildest imagination.
And if you simply don't know what to do; go within, sink into the present moment and ask Source to guide you, stay open to inspiration and take aligned action.
Be spirit lead and spontaneous, put on your mad cap and have more fun.
In your delight and wonder you will see through a lens of perfection and bliss.

191.

Divine One, in moments of doubt or unconsciousness, in moments when the ego takes over and you see life through the lens of fear, there is one simple solution.
Pause.
Pause, breathe and create space to tap into your Divinity.
Your mind may come up with a myriad of excuses as to why you cannot… but Divine One, this is the most powerful and effective thing you can do in any situation.
There is nothing that cannot wait a few moments for you to find your center.
As you find the space to pause
Close your eyes
Bring you attention to your breath
Breathe deep, in a slow and steady rhythm.
As you do that, envision a white and golden light all around you.
Become the light and remember that YOU are the light.
You are Source, God having this human experience.
If it feels in alignment with you say out loud,
"I AM God, anything is possible in this moment."
I AM Light, anything is possible in this moment.
I AM Love, anything is possible in this moment."
And as you sink into that energy make the choice to carry it with you when you open your eyes.
See the situation in front of you from the lens that you are in Fact God.
You experience the ultimate freedom when you tap into your Christ Consciousness and move forward with the knowing that everything is happening in perfect timing.
And in each moment you are loved, worthy, and held.

192.

Divine One, remember, the only truth that ever exists is the truth of the present moment, the here and now, the current moment. It is when you can walk through life in this deep state of presence that everything flows and unfolds in perfect harmony. It's in trusting that you are always held, always protected and constantly being positioned for your greatest good that you feel the Divine Support and love all around you. You see, Divine One, we are ALWAYS and FOREVER by your side, nothing you do or choose can be wrong, it is all an opportunity to learn, to grow, to deepen. So breathe in the magic of this moment right now and let all the rest fall away, knowing the timing of the Universe is Impeccable.

193.

Divine One, you are worthy here and now.
As we move into this new season of life it's time for a slowing down.
A time to breathe, to reflect, to rest, integrate and restore your senses.
It's a time to let yourSelf sink into the unknown, to let your creative juices flow and allow new ideas to begin taking root within your Soul.
This is a time of renewal, a fresh start, slow and steady in the direction of your dreams.
Society will attempt to convince you to run fast, to consume more, to create resolutions and forge new goals but it is not yet time for that, we need this winter season to simply BE with the newness of it all, to let our body catch up with the past year, and to intentionally choose what we desire to create.
Let yourself breathe, know that the slow movement and period of rest is just as important as the doing, this is the foundation of all that will unfold so be thoughtful, take your time, and remember easy does it.

194.

Divine One, playing the role of cycle breaker, light worker, leader in this lifetime is no easy feat.
You will engage in deep healing work, die to yourself thousands of times in this one body, and pick yourself up from a darkness most others can't even fathom.
And very few will understand what you have done or what you are doing.
The past generations; the parents, the grandparents, the family and friends will not see the powerful gift you are giving them, they will not understand the generations of trauma that you have alchemized.
In fact, they may even turn on you as they feel the pull back into their truth.
But Divine One, we want you to know that we see you, we understand the huge impact you are making and we know what you have sacrificed to make this world a better place.
Keep going and know you are Divinely Loved and Protected in all that you do.

195.

A channeled message for the single light workers of the world.
Divine One, you bring so much light and hope into this world.
Your presence is enough to break open hearts to the remembering of all that they are.
Your voice soothes the lost souls in this world.
Your touch shatters illusions.
And we know it hasn't always been easy, we know that because of your gifts you are often left alone to uplift and hold yourSelf the way you hold so many others.
but we want you to know the time is coming where you will meet the One who will hold you, who will see you, who will uplift you, the One who will love every part of you the way you love yourSelf and you will be able to let down your walls and do your work in this world knowing you are not alone, even in the physicality.
You are worthy of the same love you give the world Divine One, and it is coming.

196.

Divine One, you are worthy now and in every form.
How could you not be?
You Divine One, are an extension of Source Energy, an extension of pure consciousness inhabiting a human body.
Each and every action, beliefs, thought, experience is being fed back into the One Source so that it too can evolve, so that it too can experience the contrast of life on Earth.
And it's ALL YOU.
Every experience is just that, an experience that allows the Collective Consciousness to evolve.
It's the labels and weight your ego and mind put onto the experience that create suffering, that can make you feel bad and wrong or right and justified
but Divine One, it all simply IS and it can all become much lighter and joy filled when you approach this human experience with that knowing.
Walk through this day tuning into the knowing that you are an extension of Source, stay consciously connected throughout the day, finding joy, awe and wonder in every human experience and see what changes.

197.

How would you be behaving if it was already yours? If it was a sure thing? The relationship, the job, the wealth, the health? Because Divine One, it is and it will manifest in the material plane the moment you embody that knowing. It is all already yours, all available to you in this lifetime or another, it's up to you to choose it and align with it now. This is the time to believe in magic, to believe in miracles, and to live in utter human delusion. You are an extension of Source and as you tune into certain frequencies through thought, beliefs, and aligned action you materialize your desires. So truly ask yourself this…

How would I carry myself, how would I feel, how would I behave if I knew for certain that my Divine Partner is part of my life?

How would I carry myself, how would I feel, how would I behave if the money was guaranteed to be in my account?

How would I carry myself, how would I feel, how would I behave if I had perfect health?

How would I carry myself, how would I feel, how would I behave (insert desired outcome)

And as you answer those questions choose to align with the answers and live them in your every day life with full faith they are happening for you letting go of the expectations of how and when… simply know that soon it will all be yours as you act accordingly.

198.

Divine One, I know right now it may be tempting to go back into the ways of the old.
Every past memory and trigger could be surfacing now to show you how far you've come and who you no longer are.
Moving from living in the mind and simply attempting to survive to a place where you live from your heart as you consciously cultivate the world you desire to see can be startling to the system.
You are being asked to rest right now, to simply be with all that arises.
Rather than pushing through or going back to the old simply hold the light, grounded in the here and now.
Sooner than you know this entire world will look different and you will be called upon to help usher in the change.
It's all happening in perfect timing and order, it's up to you to trust the process and hold steady.

199.

Divine One, you are a force to be reckoned with.
A cosmic being on a timeless journey.
As you broaden your perspective and perception you will realize that this lifetime you are experiencing now is but one drop in the ocean on your infinite ride through space and time.
This moment right now is but the size of the thinnest needle point and while it matters a great deal to you in your human experience in the wider view it's simply another opportunity to expand and evolve the One consciousness at the Source of All.
We tell you this so you will let go, so you will live boldly, freely, in each moment.
So that you can shake it off and breathe excitement back into life.
So you can be more sincere and less serious.
So you can embody more silliness and step into your whimsical nature.
Today and all days see each moment for what it is, a glimpse of the infinite, a small moment of time in a timeless existence.
And know that YOU are ONE with it ALL.

200.

Divine One, can you be in joy today?
Can you throw your head back in silly giggles and let the wonder of this life overtake you?
Can you move forward only choosing what feels good, right, and true to you?
Can you free yourself from the expectations and the perceived limitations of your psyche and step into the limitless field of possibility that encircles your being?
Can you breathe each breath like it's your last?
Love like this is the only moment you have?
Live like you will never get this moment again?
And can you let that be enough?
Can you let that set you free?

201

Divine One, you are a masterpiece, here, now in this moment.
The way you have moved through this life, rising again and again into all that you are.
The way you have fearlessly shed the layers that no longer served you even when it meant breaking your own heart.
The way your faith never dwindles but is the constant spark leading you through the darkness.
And Divine One, it's time NOW to step into the light, to step into your fullness, opening your arms wide to receive all the gifts of the Universe.
It is your time to thrive sweet one and you are so worthy, you've always been worthy.
So breathe deep, celebrate yourSelf for all you've lived through and be at ease, for everything is about to change.

202

Divine One, like a shooting star darting across the Universe you give hope to so many.
Your essence inspires faith, wish fulfillment and possibility.
Who you are is a gift to this world.
And like the stars there is no need to try, no need to mold yourself into any other form, you are a bright and cosmic masterpiece here, now, in your original form.
It is in your shining brightly that you light up even the darkest of night, the knowing that darkness does not exist where the light shines, instead it is absorbed into the Loving Oneness of all that is.
The light doesn't try to change the darkness, it doesn't try to shame it or judge it, the light simply shines upon it fully, every single crevice and in an instant the darkness too becomes light.
That Divine One, is what you do simply by existing, you bring light to the darkest corners of the world.
Thank you.

203

Divine One, the world as we know it is changing at a drastic rate, as more and more light workers awaken to their gifts and more of the unconscious patterns are transformed by the light the old systems and structures are collapsing to make way for the new.
This is a revolutionary period to be alive on Earth, you are a part of a history that will be spoken about for centuries to come.
The New Earth is being created here and now, as more and more move away from the ways of the world and follow the call of their own heart.
In this moment; rest, attention to energetic hygiene and holding the light will ease the transition.
Soon the time will come to build, create and act and you will need both your energy and strength in optimal condition.
For now, simply be in care of your mind, body, and spirit to the best of your ability and stay open to the intuitive nudge to move.
Remember your heart has all the answers you seek.

204

Divine One, as a light worker of the world you have been called to envelop the darkness in your light.

To stand as a beacon for others in despair and to rise again and again in the frequency of Love as the world enters the new earth.

Right now you are seeing the results of nearly a century of collective wounding coming to a climax, you are seeing the darkness in these collectives brought to surface and carried out in horrific ways.

It is your job to stand in Love, free of judgment as you use your tools to help raise the vibration of the world and spark light and hope in those suffering however feels in alignment with your unique calling.

Light workers aren't passive, they are the Leader of this new earth and leaders lead through action, through voice, through energetics.

Now is the time to take a stand for love and Be the change you seek.

205

Divine One, lay down your worries and know you are always connected to the ever-loving Source within and all around you. You are a cherished cosmic being and you are needed on the Earth at this time.
As you sink into our loving embrace, feel the light rise within you, feel the inner pull of Love bringing you closer and closer into the Divine Embrace.
Know that with each step you are lovingly guided, witnessed and held. You cannot mess up what is meant for you, you cannot do anything that would separate you from the truth of all you are.
Let yourSelf breathe a little deeper as inner peace anchors within your heart and brings you back to the essence of Being.
As you stand firm in your knowing you will radiate Love and others will remember to do the same.

206

Divine One, you will always be sustained as you feed on spirit. There is an abundance of life-force energy on Earth, an abundance of the air you breathe, of the movements you make, of the people and wildlife you see.

There is an abundance of resources all around and a Divine connection ever present for you to feast upon.

As you lay your worries aside and feast on the Divine you will be held through it all.

Light encompasses the Earth now, the darkness is being purged and while it is present you have a choice in what you will partake.

Will you focus on the destruction or will you turn to light and create a ripple of love from your heart through humanity.

As you feed off the light and take aligned action you have a great impact for the better on this Earth, it is up to you to heed the call.

You have been chosen for this task and we want you to know you are not alone in this.

There are hundreds of thousands of others actively creating this new Earth and they are multitudes of Divine hosts in support of this Earthly cause.

See the abundance all around you and feed your soul. You will find the refuge you seek.

207

Divine One, you are not here to please others.
You are here to Love fully; both yourself and the world.
And through that love you change the frequency of the collective.
Love looks like unconditional acceptance.
Love looks like holding the light, Love looks like rising in your highest frequency of energy and letting others do the same in their own time and way.
There is no manipulation, no conforming, no appeasing.
Love is being You fully and utterly and letting others respond to the truth of your soul however they desire.
Being a lightworker, a leader of the New Earth is not an easy calling.
Many will tell you who and how to be, many will project their unhealed wounds onto you, many will try to manipulate or control you, to make you wrong.
And Dear One we ask you, remain in the Frequency of Love.
Let your love shine so bright that their own love and goodness is mirrored back to them and as seeds are planted, let them blossom in their own time and own way, let their hearts break open to the truth of the world and trust that they too will rise in Love.
As you focus on your own inner light and stay in alignment with your heart and soul you create ripples of change across humanity.
This is how we actively create the New Earth.

208

Divine One, you are a warrior of light, here to usher in Change and create the new earth.
You chose to come to Earth at this time, knowing the role you would play.
For the past decade you have been preparing for this, through every obstacle, every lived experience, every perceived failure you have come into alignment with the truth, the light, the way.
And Divine One, while we know this won't be easy, we do know that you are ready.
Ready to rise into all that you are, to anchor into the Earth and stay open to the new level of light you can hold.
You are different now, on a cellular level, mental level, emotional level and even physical level.
You now have the capacity to hold the highest frequencies of light even amidst so much Chaos and destruction.
This is the moment you have been waiting for.
So breathe, keep the faith and hold the light.

209

Divine One, you are the Way, the Magic, the Light. You are the One, the Truth, the Love.
It is YOU Divine One, the one you have been waiting for. The one you have been dreaming of.
You are the Channel, the Oracle, the Revolution. It is YOU.
It is time to stand in your power, to own the sacred truths that pulse within your veins, to tap into the cosmic essence of your heart and ground deep into the love and safety of the Earth Mother as you make way for the Highest Version of you.
Everything is aligning in perfect order for you to step through the womb of creation and into this new way of life.
The distance between you and your higher Self is becoming smaller and smaller and therefore the transmission of knowledge and love will feel more like they are coming from you rather than some powerful outside Source.
Trust this.
Trust yourSelf
and
Trust the Holy wisdom that pours from you.

210

Divine One, breathe and know you are held.
You are held through the joy, you are held through the pain, you are held through the sunlight and held through the rain.
In each and every moment you are held in my loving embrace.
I am with you always, within you since the beginning of time.
You can turn to me in all circumstances, let your fears and doubts be known, proclaim your desires and dreams.
Use your voice to communicate with me.
Use your heart to open to all I have to offer as we co create the reality of your dreams.
You are never alone Divine One, I am always with you.

211

Divine One, you are enough! You are stronger than you ever imagined! You are resilient, fierce, and bold.
But my love, don't forget the beauty that you hold. The grace of the divine feminine alive within you, flowing with grace and surrender. The empowered masculine leading the way.
Don't forget that you are a creator of life, a source of love, and a powerful sensual being. You, Divine One, are exactly what this world needs.
Find grace, gentleness, compassion and gratitude. Find pleasure within and for yourself, and don't be afraid to ask for what you want and need. You are more than worthy. You are more than enough.
Don't let anyone attempt to sway your beliefs or lower your self worth. Don't accept less than you deserve and don't you dare compromise yourself for the benefit of another. It's in your power and full Loving acceptance of self that you create the change this world so desperately needs.
So rise! Sink into fierce flow, embrace the journey, embody the magic, and let the miracles pour in!!!

212

Divine One, we want you to know how miraculous you are.
How your breath, your movement, you flow creates ripples of beauty and love across the cosmos.
We want you to know that as you awaken each morning the heavens open and angels look upon you in awe and wonder of the power you hold within and the grace you surround yourself with.
We want you to know that you are good and perfect just as you are and that you are always held in the safety of our loving embrace.
Feel our love today and know that LOVE is what you are.

213

Divine One, Follow your bliss.
When you follow your bliss you become magic, abundance, peace, prosperity, and love. When you step into your power, discover who you are meant to be, and live a life aligned with your soul you realize that you ARE all these things. You no longer seek abundance... You ARE abundance. When you are following your bliss, your life unfolds before you and all your wildest dreams become a reality. What kind of life sounds more inspiring to you? The kind of life in which your every move is controlled by an external circumstance or a life that you create, a life filled with passion, a life led by dreams? Choose that one.

214

Divine One, the human experience is sacred. As your heart opens to new levels of love and life, as you learn to receive deeper, open wider… You also open to the possibility of heartbreak, grief, and pain. As you align with joy each and every day you also face its polarity. And it's such an exciting thing. Because each and every experience, sensation and emotion in this human experience is a sacred one AND they don't define you. This life isn't who you are; your emotions, your circumstance, not even your body contains you. You are pure consciousness experiencing this life through a physical lens and you chose to come here. In fact you were excited to come here, to feel, to be, to connect and relate to love and to grieve. When you look at this life through a sacred lens it feels a lot less scary and gets a lot more exciting. So take a step back, breathe back into the sacred nature and let life be fun.

215

Divine One, Be Here Now. What is here now in this present moment is love.

Life unfolding for you IS Love, each and every experience, emotion, vibration, is all Sourced first and foremost from the frequency of love.

It is only your judgments of self and others that pull you away from this unified energy.

And Divine One, YOU are Love, You are Good, Your are Truth. Your mind and ego would have you think otherwise, they would have you doubt yourSelf, doubt your goodness, doubt what you really are and in doing so create further separation.

Can you consciously choose to walk in your truth today, to see that this life here and now is a miracle, that YOU are a walking and talking miracle?

Even when things feel hard and overwhelming you can come back to this presence and grace by centering into the present moment and knowing you are always held.

So breathe deep, be here now and watch the way magic is created on your behalf.

216

Divine One, now is NOT the time to fear nor divide but rather deepen into love and compassion for Self and the world.
As a leader of the New Earth you must model unconditional love, acceptance, compassion and grace.
The New Earth must be built upon the foundational TRUTHS of the Universe. Love, Integrity, Authenticity, Presence, and Grace. It is in the honoring and reverence for each moment, for each experience, for each individual and collective that you honor and uphold yourSelf.
In the coming days and months you will see many distractions, many situations that will attempt to pull you out of love and back into the illusion. We ask you to remain steadfast in your knowing and continue to create the vision of this New Earth in your mind's eye and with your aligned, heart centered action.
Rest, isolate if you must, AND REMAIN IN LOVE.

217

Divine One, Be Here Now. Breathe into the Sacred Beauty of this moment and let the rest fall away. Let go of your habits, your routines, your ways of being. Let go of the external noise and sink fully into Being. If only for a moment, listen to the tender song present in this still, soft, silence. Listen to the beating of your heart and the whispers of your soul. Let yourself dance with life, all that arises and all that falls. Ebb and flow in harmony with the Love always present and fall deeper and deeper into the beauty of this sacred existence knowing all the while what you are; pure source consciousness. Enjoy each and every moment of this human experience, of being present and connected. Enjoy every sensation both those deemed good and bad and breathe deep knowing this too shall pass. We love you so much, sweet one, and it is our desire for you to simply see the magic in true Being; it's where you become fully free.

218

Divine One, you are a cosmic being YES and you are also here now participating in this collective human experience. You are here to evolve, to learn, to grow as you experience sensations, feelings, and physical reality in a way you never have before.

Being here, now in this physical body is a sacred gift, an opportunity to awaken senses not previously known. To touch, smell, and see with such vivid awareness, to open to a world previously unknown. To participate in humanity and learn through relationships. This is all a part of what it means to be human. Both the beauty and the pain of it all is a gift to be cherished. To see the world through eyes of awe, wonder and excitement as if it is the first time every time. To be enamored by physical sensations both ones filled with pleasure and ones filled with pain. This is what it is to be fully alive in this dimension and believe it or not you were truly excited to come to Earth and be present for this great collective healing taking place. So sink into gratitude for the here and now and live fully alive as you participate in this human experience.

219

Divine One, it was your intention when you came to Earth to be a part of the human experience and therefore a part of humanity. Right now humanity is failing and it is your job as a collective of spiritual beings on Earth to come together and create change for the better. To rise in love and integrate the darkness and the light, to envision a better world for tomorrow and be the change you want to see in your everyday life. It's time to tune into your soul, into your sacred essence and discover the important role you play in the evolution of the Earth. As humanity heals heaven on earth is created and it starts with you, each and everyone of you have done the Inner Work necessary to cultivate inner harmony and now it is time to let that harmony ripple across the earth to bring healing to all. As we rise in love together, united as One everything changes.

220

Divine One, your prayers are being answered. Every whisper of your heart has been heard, every longing in your soul has been realized. Live this truth, feel it in your bones, know it in your soul and soften your heart to receive all that is meant for you and more. We have watched you courageously move forward through this world and these experiences with hope in your heart. We've watched you traverse the Earth and embody the love you seek and now Divine One, it is time to receive. In each and every moment you are being granted the answers to your prayers, simply open the eyes of your heart and reveal them standing before you. This message is confirmation that your prayers are being answered in the perfect time and the perfect way. As you continue to make them known you need but have faith and they will find their way into your waking reality. Know this, believe this, live this and it will be.

221

Divine One, it's time to experience deep and lasting joy, miracles, and reap the fruits of your labor. We are so proud of you for the work you have been doing on yourSelf, you are quite literally changing the frequency of the collective consciousness. Good job. And now it's time for pleasure, ease, abundance and joy as you continue to move forward in the creation of heaven on Earth. We ask you now to sink into visualization of all you desire to see present not only for yourself but for this glorious planet as a whole. Humanity is awakening to the destructive patterns of the old and more hope that ever is present on this planet. Hope that feeds movement and instills inspiration for change and an inner revolution of the heart. By being in your joy, by allowing creative passion to flow through you and by visualizing a new type of world in your divine mind you will create lasting and positive change. For now, let that be enough sweet one, it only gets better from here.

222

Divine One, this earthly experience is filled with experiences of every kind; it was meant to be. You are here to expand, to experience, to evolve. There is a common misconception that it's meant to be all sunshine and roses, that happiness is the answer and you have to feel good in all moments. That is simply not the case and actually quite counter to everything you signed up for when you made your journey to Earth. You see, Divine One, you came here as a fragment of Source Consciousness under the premise that you would experience a vast array of emotions both "good and bad" both "pleasurable and Painful" both light and dark. You chose this knowing that with each experience you and therefore the wholeness of Source would evolve and expand into deeper depths and great knowing. You came here for the Evolution of the Soul. Your pain, doubts, fears, and darkness are not something to run from or avoid but rather parts of this human experience to be embraced and cherished, and as you do you harness even more life force energy to create more of what you desire. So today we ask you to redefine your views of pain and open to every sensation and experience available to you now. From there you can create your wildest dreams and live a truly free life on Earth.

THANK YOU

Divine One, thank you for partaking in this journey, for feasting upon these words and this energy and allowing yourself to expand into the fullness of all that you are. This journey called life is a magical one meant to be felt, experienced and opened to fully. As you move forward in your journey it is my hope that you will remember your sacred essence, you will walk this Earth like the magical being you are and own your power, your potential, your fullness. In the following pages you will find a beautiful prayer for humanity, one I sink into on a nightly basis to bring healing to myself and the world as well as resources and ways to connect as you continue down your path. It's been an honor to walk with you as you opened into the remembering of all that you are and if our paths don't cross again on this earthly plane know that I love you, I see you, I am you.

Xoxo
Nikyla Maria

A SACRED PRAYER FOR HUMANITY

Divine Source of All That Is,
I stand here, grounded in the essence of my shared humanity,
Connected to the sacred earth, and uplifted by the light of higher consciousness.
I honor the breath of life that flows through every soul,
Knowing that we are all connected, brothers and sisters on this journey of existence.

I awaken to the truth of my divine nature,
Understanding that within me lies the power to create, to heal, and to transform.
I embrace the fullness of my human experience—
The joy and the sorrow, the love and the pain—
For within these contrasts, I find the sacred dance of life.

I seek the wisdom to see beyond the illusions of separation,
To know that we are all threads in the same cosmic tapestry,
Woven together by the hands of love and compassion.
I walk this earth with humility,
Honoring the sacred in every step, in every being I encounter.

In moments of darkness, I remember the light within,
And in times of fear, I find courage in the depths of my heart.
My heart is open to receive the divine guidance that leads me to my highest self,
And my actions reflect the truth of our interconnectedness.

I pray for healing—healing of the wounds that divide us,
Healing of the earth that sustains us,
And healing of the spirit that longs to return to wholeness.

I am a vessel of peace,
Anchoring love in a world that often forgets its sacred origins.
And I live in a way that honors the sacredness of every life,
Knowing that in each act of kindness, I uplift the entire world.

So it is, and so it shall be.
Amen.

BONUS RESOURCES AND COMMUNITY

Check out this link to connect with Nikyla Maria

https://linktr.ee/nikylamaria

ABOUT THE AUTHOR

Nikyla Maria is a recognized expert in self-mastery and inner child healing, known for her transformative work with clients worldwide. She is a published author, divine channel, speaker, and creator of the popular Inner Child Oracle Deck. With over 15 years of experience in leadership, education, and performance, she has guided countless creatives, thought leaders, and industry stars to their next level of personal and professional growth. Nikyla has touched countless lives with her teachings, helping others awaken to their inherent divinity and live in alignment with their highest selves.

Her journey in self-mastery is deeply rooted in her own life experience working through trauma and bringing light to the darkness mixed with her academic background, holding a master's degree in Educational Leadership and Curriculum Design. In addition to her academic achievements, Nikyla is a certified Master Healer, Trauma-Trained Internal Family Systems (IFS) Expert, and Licensed Holistic Practitioner. Her unique combination of expertise has allowed her to develop high-performance tools and master mindset strategies that have consistently led her clients to greater productivity, creativity, self-discipline and a more heart-centered life.

Nikyla's work is not just about individual transformation; it is a call to collective awakening. Her teachings inspire a global community to elevate their consciousness, honor their sacred journey, and contribute to the healing and evolution of humanity. Through her teachings, programs, and published works like "I Am the Villain," she invites others to embrace their authentic power, heal their inner wounds, and rise to their highest potential. Her mission is to guide humanity toward a more conscious, compassionate, and empowered existence, one person at a time.

In addition to her one-on-one work, Nikyla has hosted healing retreats across the globe and has developed a series of spiritual tools and resources, including her renowned Inner Child Oracle Cards. These cards, accompanied by a comprehensive guidebook, have become a powerful resource for those seeking to heal and connect with their inner child, with rave reviews from users who have experienced profound shifts in their lives.

Nikyla's work is a testament to her commitment to helping others reclaim their true selves and live lives filled with purpose, joy, and inner peace. Whether through her writings, teachings, speaking engagements, or her podcast *Embodied Divinity*, she continues to inspire and empower individuals on their journey of self-discovery, leading them down the path of awakening, guiding them to remember who they truly are and live in alignment with the divine purpose they carry within.

Her creations are a living embodiment of her belief in the sacredness of the human experience and the potential for divine transformation within us all. She has an unwavering commitment to helping others realize their fullest potential and contribute to a more conscious and compassionate world.

For more about Nikyla's work, including her podcast "Embodied Divinity" and her ongoing creative projects, visit her website or connect with her on social media using the link in the book's bonus section.

www.ingramcontent.com/pod-product-compliance
Lightning Source LLC
Chambersburg PA
CBHW051327110526
44582CB00003B/73